Everyday Happy

365 ways to a better you

Everyday Happy

Happy

365 ways to a better you

Jenny Hare

Illustrated by Michelle Tilly

spruce

An Hachette UK Company
First published in Great Britain in 2009 by Spruce
a division of Octopus Publishing Group Ltd
2–4 Heron Quays, London E14 4JP.
www.octopusbooks.co.uk
www.octopusbooksusa.com

Distributed in the US and Canada for Octopus Books USA
c/- Hachette Book Group USA
237 Park Avenue
New York NY 10017.

Produced by **Bookworx**
Editorial Jo Godfrey Wood, **Design** Peggy Sadler

ISBN 13 978-1-84601-332-4
ISBN 10 1-84601-332-1

A CIP catalogue record for this book is available from the British Library.

Printed and bound in China

10 9 8 7 6 5 4 3 2 1

Contents

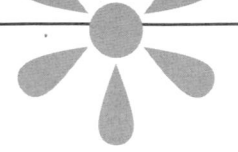

Introduction

In all its forms, from the quietest contentment through appreciation to the most exuberant joy, happiness is a truly brilliant thing.

Is it possible for you to encourage it into your life? Very much so! A positive attitude is a decision that you can make every day, over and over again. Any number of things, like the suggestions in this book, can bring about gladness and happiness. But they'll only do their stuff if you help them along by willingly giving them a go.

Sometimes happiness is quite spontaneous, of course. But actively practicing happiness feels great, too, for when you take control of your own life and your own emotions you'll find that it's immensely satisfying and enriching.

But what of loss, bereavement and a myriad of other sorrows? We all have our share of these things in our lives and at these times grief may become our whole being. But the thought of happiness past can be a raft to help us through dark days, as can a readiness to heal and, in time, to welcome happiness back.

And what about being lucky? Again, it's lovely when we are, but chance wins and other haphazard good fortunes can give only a temporary high.

Deep, lasting happiness comes from a personal approach to life that nurtures happiness inside and around us. In time, it becomes a habit and it's simply the best!

Dip into this book whenever you need some inspiration and also to remind you to practice being happy every single day of your life, at least some of the time.

I wish you much happiness. Most of all, I wish for you the realization that your life is a miracle and a great gift. It is. Enjoy!

With love to you,

Jenny Hare

How to use this book

If you've bought this book as part of your plan for the New Year, that's fine, but if you've picked it up at some time during the middle of the year, don't worry. It will still work for you. You don't have to start it on New Year's Day; you can start any time you feel like it during the year. Just turn to Day 1 and work your way through the days in order. You will find that the months have either 30 or 31 days to reflect the real year, so you might want to match the month you're in with one that has the correct number of days on offer (the first month has 31 days).

At the end of every month you'll find a page for assessing how you're getting on. This is just an opportunity to think about what you've read and whether any of the ideas are working for you. There's also a space here to write down your thoughts and think about how you're getting on. Run out of writing space? Turn to the final pages of the book and you'll find more pages to continue any important personal notes.

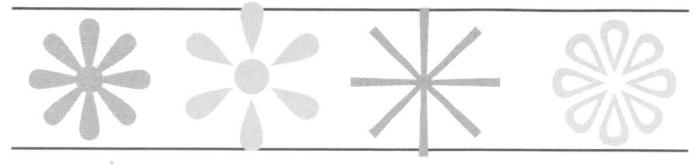

Do something really active

Feeling a bit down? Try doing something really active and proactive. You might go for a run, pop round to see an old friend, wash the kitchen floor or start up a new project. Even just making a decision to do something specific will help you to feel happier.

Once you get going, using up energy will generate even more energy, and instantly your body will respond with endorphins (feel-good chemicals). Not only do you feel good when you are being active, but afterwards you'll bask in the satisfaction of having been active.

How many small physical luxuries have you experienced today? Count them up. Did you wake up in a comfortable, warm bed and have plenty of hot water for your shower? Did your transport run on schedule, did you have a nice lunch and how was your welcome hot drink when you arrived home again?

Instead of taking these small things for granted, take a moment to appreciate each one to the full. Noticing how fortunate you are in so many diverse ways creates a sense of richness and wellbeing in your life. And feeling glad and being thankful feels fantastic. Noticed and appreciated, small pleasures contribute hugely to your everyday happiness.

Instant happy

TAKE A LONG, HOT BATH

The next time you run yourself a bath, enjoy every moment: the lovely hot water, the depth of it, your bubble bath, the candles you've lit around it, your nice glass of wine. Think how lucky you are.

11

Do you ever get that sluggish feeling? It may hit you after lunch, during the late afternoon or after an intense work session, when you experience a sudden feeling of exhaustion, which can make you feel a bit down.

When you get these spells, it's worth assessing what the best plan of action is. Pushing yourself to do some more work can create a new surge of energy that feels great. Or perhaps you actually do need to rest. If so, respect it and relax. Your work will benefit when it is time to start again. Decide whether to push yourself or to take a break when you flag. Practicing listening to your gut feelings in this way pays dividends as you'll feel happily in tune with your body and mind.

Go for a mini-break

Take a mini-break; it's enjoyable, relaxing and reviving and almost as much of a tonic as a proper holiday.

The process of preparing and packing, even for a day-trip or a night away, gives you almost the same amounts of enjoyable anticipation as a longer break. The mini-holiday itself refreshes and relaxes you. If you're with a partner, it's romantic and intimate. And it's great to get home, too. What's not to like? It's all-round holiday happiness.

Instant happy

TAKE DESK-BREAKS
Leave your desk. Sit, or preferably, lie down, and shut your eyes. Think of something that is nothing to do with work for ten minutes (a special picture you like or a recent holiday). When your mind wanders, redirect it back to your chosen focus. When you open your eyes you will feel refreshed again.

Phone someone today who might love to hear from you. Don't wait for a reason to do it, just call them and say you were thinking of them, or that you wanted to hear their voice and catch up.

Keep your voice light. Put expression and love into your voice as you say hello and revel in the surprise and pleasure you hear in their response. The more spontaneous calls you make for friendship's sake, the more you'll receive. Don't do it just to get a return call, though. Do it primarily because it feels so good both to make contact and to give the other person pleasure. Create double happiness: call a friend, make yourself happy and make her happy, too.

orgive someone for something today. Bitterness and resentment, however mild, can sabotage your personal happiness. Letting go of such feelings frees you up to be light-hearted and happy.

Imagine yourself shaking the negativity off you and seeing it fall away. Forgiving someone doesn't mean that you condone what they did; it simply means you're no longer going to judge and let anger eat you up. Remind yourself that the other person's conscience is not your story and give yourself a hug for being so reasonable, sensible and mature.

Instant happy

PRACTICE FORGIVENESS
Think 'I forgive them' as often as you need to, to keep your forgiveness current. You'll be surprised how much better you feel.

Think first

REMIND YOURSELF
If you're the kind of person who tends to speak first and think later, try this out: whenever you feel an impulse to speak out, count to ten before opening your mouth.

Think before you act and say or do the right thing at the right time. Often the idea of what the right thing is comes to you too late.

Focus on the moment and ask yourself what would be a positive action right now. Paying attention to what you could do gives you the chance to do something beneficial, before it's too late. Knowing you've made a difference to someone else's day by a thoughtful action or some careful words is guaranteed to give you a warm glow. Light up your own and others' lives by saying something kind, useful or inspiring.

Today's the first day

Whatever your mood is right now, take a second to feel a rush of excitement at the thought that today is a new, fresh beginning.

Living this new beginning, how would you like your day to be? Yes, there'll probably be the same need to work, the usual chores to do at home, the same not-perfect people around you. But, hey, just keep the feeling of a fresh start with you all day and see how it automatically brightens up your approach to life and makes a beneficial difference to all aspects of it. Put some extra oomph into being positive, and you'll be sure to notice the difference very soon.

Instant happy

LIVE IN THE PRESENT
Make the present moment a fresh start. Now!

Delay some of today's small pleasures and enjoy the extra anticipation this gives you. Even something as mundane as a cup of coffee will be all the more delicious if you wait a while for it and are able to look forward to it. Instead of something commonplace, it becomes a treat, a gift to yourself, a reward for work well done.

Delayed gratification will also heighten your senses, so it's a way both of adding to, and heightening, pleasure. And exercising will-power feels good, too. Instead of taking a 'must have it now' attitude, decide when you are going to have something and be glad to wait for it.

Is your path right?

At least once a month check out with yourself as to how you're feeling about your life. If it's pretty well set on the course you want, be glad and appreciate it. Or perhaps you'll find you need to make a few adjustments.

Just noticing and bringing awareness to an issue that needs attention will set you thinking how to go about making changes, and your subconscious will help you to get back on track, too. Notice how you're doing. This puts you in touch with your needs and that connection feels really good.

Today's thought

KEEP A JOURNAL
Use your daily journal to assess the way your life is going.

19

Revel in sounds

LISTEN TO BIRDSONG

Notice all the different kinds of birdsong early in the morning. Be glad that it's there to be heard and that you can hear it.

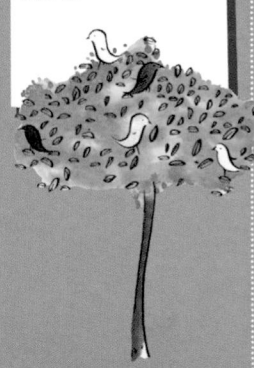

Sound is often the first thing we notice when we wake up. This is probably because we've been woken up by it and feel we'd like to linger in bed a little longer. Choose to let the sound make you happy rather than annoyed.

How? It's easy. Instead of trying to block sounds out or complaining about them, put a positive spin on them. Be glad for the gift of hearing and for the early link with the world it provides. Smile and send blessings to the people or animals around you. Give thanks for the new day. Listen with love in your heart. Nurture your sense of humor and enjoy feeling connected with the world and the life you've woken up to.

Notice all the goodness in the world and it will lift your spirits. It's so easy to get lost in gloom and doom. The news and media generally tend to concentrate on bad news. It's more sensational and it holds the public's attention. As is often stated, 'Bad news sells newspapers.'

Keep a sense of perspective. There are huge amounts of good fortune, happiness, love and positivity around you, both close at hand and in the wider world. Look out for the goodness and you'll see it's not delusional to believe in it; it's all around you.

Remembering and recognizing the amazing wealth of goodness in people counters cynicism and gives you a wonderful feeling of uplift.

MAKE PLANS

Think of something you'd like to do that would improve your health; something you'd enjoy. Make an appointment today to start the activity. Write it down in your journal.

How's your health today? Feeling good? Keep up the good work with lots of tender loving care. If your health's not so hot, then you need to give yourself even more TLC. Also make definite plans as to how you can give your body the best chance to gain full health and become fitter.

Realizing there's a lot you can do to promote your health stops you feeling helpless, as though you are at the mercy of fate, and fills you with hope and positive help instead. Notice how you are and do something to enhance your health today.

Feeling a little disgruntled? Pay attention to this feeling. Denying a negative emotion will let it flourish rather than banishing it, so confront it the minute you notice it.

Instead of saying 'I'm not angry, depressed or frustrated', when deep down you know that you are, admit it to yourself and also to someone else in your life, so that it becomes real. Negating negativity makes it all the more persistent. Recognition of a bad mood dislodges its command over you. Instantly you will feel a bit better. It also gives you the chance to think about the causes and address them. You can then draw in positivity instead, and that gives your happiness a firm hold again.

Today's thought

FEELING NEGATIVE?
If you feel negative say:
'What's this about?'
You'll find the answers
and strategies you need.

Watch how you walk

IMAGINE A MIRROR

Visualize a full-length mirror in front of you, or someone you love watching you. See how you immediately straighten up and move more gracefully. It feels so good.

Tread, don't trudge. How you walk around can hugely uplift your mood and having a spring in your step can really improve your frame of mind.

Don't slouch. Carry yourself proudly, as though you're walking on air; you'll feel as though you really are. Walk tall, step out confidently, lift your chest up from your tum, your chin from your throat. The minute you improve your posture your outlook lifts, too. And if you swing your legs from your hips instead of using your whole body to lift them, you'll not only look like a fashion model but also feel stylish into the bargain.

It's easy to let others, or yourself, sabotage your ideas and dreams. But they'll only come to fruition if you have a determined belief in them and your ability to take them foward. So think positively and work out possibilities and plans to help them on their way.

Sometimes new projects develop a life of their own and take off really quickly, which is fine. Mostly, though, they need ongoing faith in yourself as well as them, with persistence and courage in equal measure.

It feels amazing. Go for it! Hold fast to a great idea that you think has mileage. Putting your thoughts and actions behind your dream sets happiness free.

Today's thought

START A BOOK OF DREAMS

Acquire a special notebook, perhaps with a pretty cover, and make a point of listing all your hopes and dreams. This makes them become real. Keep it handy and refer to it often.

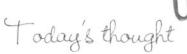

Today's thought

A GOOD RECIPE
Never trouble trouble
until trouble troubles
you; it's a good recipe
for happiness.

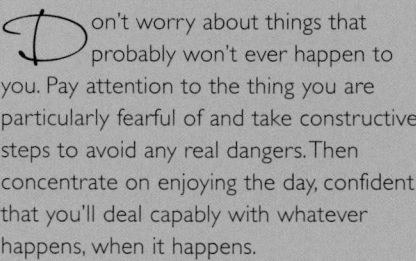

Don't worry about things that probably won't ever happen to you. Pay attention to the thing you are particularly fearful of and take constructive steps to avoid any real dangers. Then concentrate on enjoying the day, confident that you'll deal capably with whatever happens, when it happens.

Living your life as though you are constantly being threatened is self-defeating. Instead, see fear as an ally to warn you. Dealing with it sensibly stops you becoming obsessive about it. Once the warning's dealt with the fear will subside, leaving you free to be cheerful and relaxed.

Reserve plenty of time to be on time. It's pleasing and it lets you be stress-free. If you're always rushing to meet appointments or you complete tasks in too much of a hurry, you'll be constantly stressed and happiness will be harder for you to achieve.

The feeling of getting somewhere in good time is extremely satisfying. It helps you to feel efficient and professional. And it respects other people's time, too. After all, people need you to appreciate them and the efforts they've made.

It's wonderful to know you've got ample time to do a job well. Punctuality prompts personal poise and is always pleasing for yourself and others around you.

Instant Happy

CALCULATE YOUR JOURNEY LENGTHS

Work out roughly how long your journey is going to take, then add an extra 15 minutes. If you have to kill time at the other end, it won't matter.

However busy you are, remember to make the effort to schedule in some quiet time just for you. Don't think of it as selfish or unjustified; it isn't. It's good for your soul, your mental balance and your ability to be both efficient and loving, in fact for your general happiness. Your work and everyone around you will benefit.

Aim for at least half an hour, but even a few minutes is better than nothing. What you do is up to you. You might doze, read or nip into a place of worship or a park to have a few quiet moments all to yourself. What's important is that you still your mind in the hustle and bustle of everyday life.

Stimulants can make you feel edgy and reduce your potential 'happy' moments. So consider any caffeine-containing drinks and other chemical stimulants you consume and choose water or a soothing herbal tea, such as peppermint or chamomile, instead.

Rather than risking making you feel over-active and even anxious, these caffeine-alternatives will boost your feelings of wellbeing and calm, helping your inner happiness to stay steadily with you throughout the day.

In principle, be good to your body and mind by imbibing feel-good drinks rather than the ones that seem to pep you up, only to make you feel edgy and hyperactive afterwards.

Instant happy

CHAMOMILE AND CATMINT TEA
Put one teaspoon of chamomile and one teaspoon dried catmint into a teapot. Cover with boiling water. Infuse for 15 minutes before drinking.

29

WALK ROUND THE BLOCK

Go outside and walk briskly round the block for ten minutes. You'll feel refreshed and revived, and ready to start work again.

We carry out tasks far better if we take regular breaks. Frequent breaks aren't skiving, they're energizing and essential for your wellbeing. So don't sit at your desk or stick at any task for hours at a time. Get up, move about and do something different for a while. Every 40 minutes or so, take a few minutes out to relax; even walking about the room or gazing out of window will feel good and give you a break.

Longer breaks mid-morning and afternoon and a proper lunch break complement your day. Your efficiency and creativity will soar and you'll enjoy your work all the more.

hat you eat affects your moods as well as your body, so it's important to get to know the benefits of various foods so you can choose your meals and snacks with thought and care. This not only gives you a selection of delicious tastes to enjoy, but all the nutrients you need to keep yourself healthy and happy.

Occasional, small junk-food treats, such as crisps and chocolate, are fine, but try to limit them to one or two modest portions per day. As a general guideline, include plenty of fruit and vegetables (five portions a day is good to aim for) in your diet, some protein and carbohydrates and choose whole foods when you can.

day 23 | *Leave your work at work*

Instant happy

CHANGE GEAR

Try changing into casual, comfortable clothes when you get home. This will help you relax and leave your work day behind. This is particularly effective if your work clothes are somewhat formal.

Form the habit of leaving your work behind you when you leave your workplace. Try not to take it home with you. Keep your home life separate so that you can relax and enjoy your leisure time, family and friends to the full.

Your leisure time is an oasis of happiness for you to relax in. With no work worries and tensions invading your privacy, it's a special time, just for you and yours. A proper break from work also replenishes your energy and inspiration, so you'll feel restored and ready for work again tomorrow.

What time of year is it? Maybe you are so busy that you haven't really noticed. Observe which season you are in and feel its magic by taking a walk in the park or countryside.

Autumn? Enjoy its fruitfulness and have fun scrunching through the richly colored leaves.

Winter? Look at the amazing shapes of the trees without their clothing of leaves.

Spring? Thrill to the sight of snowdrops, crocuses and the other early flowers.

Summer? Wallow in the abundance of flowers and foliage. Feel your spirits leap as you enjoy nature's marvelous pageant of changing colors, scents and shapes.

Instant happy

SEASONAL REMINDERS

Collect small items from nature, take them home to put on display as a reminder of the season. Why not pick up some golden, crispy leaves the next time you go for a walk?

33

THINK BEFORE YOU SHOUT
Do this and you'll calm down and come up with a better strategy for both yourself and the problem, leaving your inner happiness undamaged.

Ever experienced that feeling when someone irritates you and you feel your anger surging? Anger is a sort of self-indulgence that can be very destructive, both to your relationships with others and to yourself.

Decide right now that you won't let your anger rise to the surface the next time someone pushes your buttons. Instead, pause to think how love would act in your shoes, to everyone's benefit. Anger used to lash out just makes everything worse, so choose a calm, constructive way to deal with the situation. Or walk away from the problem for a while. That could be the solution in itself, giving you time to relax and get things back into perspective. Or, if something does need to be acted on, a good way of responding will come to you.

Fish out a happy notion

Whenever you feel washed out, imagine delving into your bag and fishing out a happy notion. It could be a loved one's smile or something wonderful that once happened. Or it could be a piece of wisdom you carry around with you. Feel the warm hug of happiness it gives you.

Go to a live 'happening'

Have fun taking your pick from listings of live events in newspapers or on the Internet. Whatever you attend, enjoy the anticipation beforehand. Be a positive member of the audience, cheerfully showing your interest in, and appreciation of, the event as it unfolds.

Happiness loves simplicity. Simple solutions, the heart of the matter, love; these things are all there, all the time, right under your nose.

It's so easy, though, to go charging down all sorts of complicated routes and make the simplest things into convoluted puzzles and problems. Look at what's really important and you'll cut through all the loops and tangles and get straight to the heart of happiness. In matters large and small, look for the nub of the problem. It feels so good to live simply.

In character, in manners, in style, in all things the supreme excellence is simplicity.

Henry Longfellow

*L*oving yourself doesn't mean being narcissistic, arrogant or self-centered. It's really all about getting on with, and liking, yourself.

Maybe you don't always find yourself so terribly likeable? Of course not; you're only human after all! But that gives you the immediate, ongoing chance to be kinder and/or better in some other way and be the person you want to be.

Today's thought

ACCEPT YOURSELF
Do your best, be your best and love the way you are.

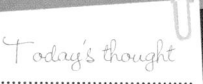

Today's thought

BOY MEETS GIRL
Whether you are Mars
or Venus, love your
differences.

Are men and women so very different? You bet they are! It isn't just because of the way we have been nurtured; it's genetic, so the sexes always will be different.

So, next time someone of the opposite sex mystifies or frustrates you with behavior that's so very untypical of your own gender, understand the fundamental differences between you, smile wryly and shrug your shoulders. That way it won't bug you and you'll merrily say, 'Vive la difference!'

Understood and accepted, our respective character traits are interesting and can complement each other happily.

Laughing out loud is an instant way to feel happy and goodhearted laughter is an instant happiness that shines on everyone around you. So look around and think of something to make you laugh. Your sense of fun will brighten up everyone around you.

In a hospital clinic waiting room, for example, you might notice the good effect cheerful, upbeat receptionists and medics have on everyone there. If they are cheery and smiley, not loud, just quietly amusing, it creates a relaxing atmosphere, making a potentially scary hospital wait into a lighter-hearted time.

Instant happy

INSTANT LAUGHTER
How many people can you make laugh with your laughter today?

Whether you tried out several ideas this month or just one, you might like to reflect on what you chose to try and why, and if it worked for you.

1. How many activities did you try this month?

- 1–3 activities ☐
- 4–10 activities ☐
- 11–20 activities ☐
- 21–31 activities ☐

2. How many did you repeat several times in the month?

- 1–3 activities ☐
- 4–10 activities ☐
- 11–20 activities ☐
- 21–31 activities ☐

3. Which activities had a positive effect on your mood this month?

Use the page opposite to make notes about what worked for you and what didn't.

Notes, jottings and thoughts

Don't get involved

> *If it ain't broke,*
> *don't fix it.*
>
> Anon

Be aware if, like many of us, you have a tendency to get over-involved and attempt to organize other people, even when nothing really needs to be done.

If you like to control things and you have leadership skills, this is great. But it's important to use them only when they are really needed. Most of the time people and situations potter along just fine, sorting any snags or quirks out for themselves. Keep your eyes open and be sensitive to whether your input is really helpful or whether it is unnecessary and even unwelcome.

Standing back and letting be is often the best recipe for a happy outcome all round, yourself included.

Give a warm touch

A warm touch could be all it takes to make someone you know feel better. With your touch, show someone you feel for them and understand. Experience a warmth reach out from you to them.

Keep your touch light as some people feel uncomfortable with physical contact. You could hold their hand or just place your hand over it or put a gentle hand on their shoulder or knee.

Touch is a moment's connection that transmits your solidarity and support. It says, more than words can; that you're there for them. Touch can conduct healing, love and inspiration. It's powerful, empathetic and joins you in a wave of quiet happiness.

Instant happy

CONTACT
Today, resolve to make simple physical contact with at least one person; maybe an ordinary handshake, but perhaps even a hug.

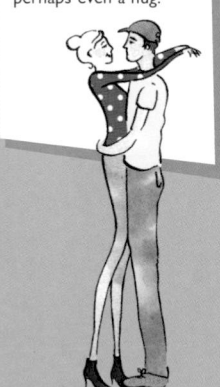

Happiness is an art, a habit, a knack that gets easier and easier with practice, until it's second nature. However humans are sensitive, vulnerable, emotional creatures and however cheerful and contented you become, your moods vary. When they dip and you mourn the disappearance of happiness, remember that it isn't a destination, once reached, that you can stay in.

Happiness is certainly a path you can choose, but sometimes you'll stray or be pushed off it, or lose sight of it in confusion. Have faith that you'll find it again. You will. Don't expect to be happy constantly, but know you are on a path full of chances for happiness and many periods of contentment or great joy.

> Happiness isn't a destination; it's a journey.
>
> Anon

Put on some make-up

Try wearing a little make-up, even if you don't normally or you don't feel it's worth it if you're not going out. Make-up isn't just for others to see; it's for you. It needn't be a lot, as even a subtle touch can transform your spirits.

Even if you're not really expecting to see another soul all day, putting on a little make-up signals the love that you can feel toward yourself. It's like a little treat that you can give to yourself. It's good to look in the mirror and think, 'There, that's better.' Maybe you feel you're gilding the lily when your face is lovely anyway? Sure, why not? What's important is that a little sparkle adds a glow to your self-esteem all day long.

Instant happy

KEEP IT MINIMAL
You needn't do the full works. Some lipstick or blusher, for instance, is enough to make a difference.

Indulge yourself and sink happily into the latest novel by one of your preferred writers, as soon as it's published. Splash out on the hardback version, just this one time.

Knowing that you're one of the book's first readers will give you an added feeling of closeness to the author. It's also exciting to be one of the first to discover and review a new book and fun to compare your thoughts with the reviewers in the press.

Materially, there's something very special and pleasing about a brand-new book: it looks, smells and feels especially good to handle. Enjoy the quality of the paper, the hard cover and the dust jacket.

Be spontaneous

Try to be more spontaneous in your life. However content you are with your usual lifestyle, saying 'yes' to a new suggestion can create six sets of happiness.

1. The instant extra buzz as you enjoy the surprise of the idea.
2. The additional interest of considering it positively.
3. The pleasure of saying 'yes!'
4. The excitement of actually following it through.
5. The satisfaction of having done it.
6. The ongoing glow of the new memory you've made.

So try to say 'yes' more often and reap the benefits in so many ways.

Instant Happy

GIVE THANKS
Every day appreciate
your meals, your clothes
and your home. Bask in
this warm feeling.

If you are lucky enough to have some nice things, you should enjoy them as much as you can. Jewelry, for example, can be a source of great pleasure and pride.

But precious things can also cause worry. Perhaps you avoid wearing certain pieces because you are concerned about losing them. Try not to waste time and emotion being anxious about things and beware of being jealous of other people's.

Realize, instead, what is truly valuable, in material terms, in your life. Think about what is essential to you in your life. When it comes right down to it, all you need is shelter, food and warmth. The rest is luxury, to be enjoyed.

Happiness is not being a victim. No one can bully or shame you unless you allow them to, by giving them your power. Hold on to your power with all your might. Sometimes just showing that you're not giving way emotionally is all it takes to gain others' respect. Or you may need to seek help to confront and root out emotional or physical threats.

Fear not! Help is at hand. It doesn't just feel good to stand up for yourself; it feels amazingly good. Personal power. Go for it! Stand firm against victimization and feel how good it is to be free of it.

Over? Let it go!

He who binds to
himself a joy
Does the winged
life destroy.
He who kisses
the joy as it flies
Lives in eternity's
sunrise.

William Blake

If a good relationship has run its course, let it go gracefully. Yes, you'll miss it and if it was something very, very precious to you it will hurt a lot. Grieving the loss fully may take time, but eventually you will heal and your sorrow will fade.

It helps the miracle of healing to be glad and thankful for the joy you were lucky enough to experience. Even if it's too painful now, in the immediate aftermath of your loss, in time remember and enjoy again, in your mind, the good times that you had together.

Refuse to get bogged down by bitterness and regret and give thanks for the love and fun you had, knowing happiness will soon come back to you again.

Give compliments

Say wonderful things to your loved ones. See how many lives you can light up with a genuine compliment. Watch the spark of pleasure you light and count the smiles and sparkly eyes. You'll be surprised at how easy it is to find something really nice to say, and mean it, and it will light up your day, too.

Hear a child laughing

There are few things as wondrous and charming as the laughter of a little child. The expression of pure delight is doubly entrancing as the sound is enchanting and shows the child's developing sense of fun. You'll laugh, too, it's totally infectious. Yes, a child's laughter is a jewel of happiness beyond price.

day 43 — Breathe deeply

If you are going through a time of particular anxiety, the beneficial effect of steady, slow breathing is even quicker if you cup your hands over your nose. As you concentrate for a few minutes on your breathing, the rhythm and increased intake of carbon dioxide induce a feeling of calm and deep happiness.

Feel happiness flow through you. It helps to imagine, as you breathe out, that any negative feelings are rushing out of you and that you are breathing in positivity and love. Slowing and deepening your breathing is a quick, practical way to reduce stress and restore your sense of inner harmony.

U-turns are OK

Even self-assured people sometimes have to make U-turns; we are all fallible. It's important that you don't feel you must persevere with something just because you said you would. Although it's good to follow through with your decisions, if you realize that one of yours has turned out to be wrong, it's best to admit it to yourself, and anyone else involved, and work out what the best course of action is.

Changing your mind takes courage and, when it's the right thing to do, it will make you happy. Reverse a decision if you know in your heart that you must. It will enable you to relax, knowing you've done what's right.

Instant happy

UMBRELLA VISUALIZATION
With eyes closed, imagine that you have your umbrella up and that people's harsh words are raining down on it, but they cannot touch you.

Steer clear of lashing out in retaliation at someone who is critical of you. Revenge may feel sweet when you are in the moment, but it can quickly turn sour, making you feel crabby and uncomfortable. Better by far to smile at, or ignore, their words as, then or later, you quietly consider them. If you can learn something from them, do so and be glad of the opportunity. But if mistaken, over-harsh or downright unnecessary, shrug them off and tell yourself firmly that it's not fair and that you're not taking it on board.

By refusing to rise to other people's judgments, whether or not they're justified, you'll withstand the knocks of criticism and your confidence and happiness will remain undamaged.

Go for a ramble

Rambling is a joy. Rambling walks and rambling thoughts are a real pleasure and can be inspirational in your daily life. You could take a walk with no planned destination or route. Or you could simply sit quietly and see what comes into your mind and where your musing takes you. You could of course combine the two!

The joy of rambling is that you experience freshness, interest and, sometimes, excitement or fun, as you see new sights and have new ideas. Rambling is both relaxing and invigorating.

Instant happy

BOOTS BY THE DOOR

Keep your walking boots by your front door or in your car; somewhere where you always see them. You'll be constantly reminded how important it is for you to go rambling, in body or mind.

Have a weekly treat

Have a treat that's just for you, at least once a week. It should be something that's purely for your own pleasure and no one else's. It could, for example, be something arty or cultural, or a physical pleasure, or something connected with a hobby, whatever you think would be enjoyable and feel fulfilling, to you alone.

The happiness an outing provides will make you more willing to take part in the usual hustle and bustle at work and in family life. With your soul replenished, you will be able to enjoy all of your life full on. You'll soon find that your whole life will receive an infusion of happiness and energy.

Crack a joke

*W*atch out for the opportunity to make a quip. It could be something ironic, ridiculous, witty, a clever pun or some other amusing play on words. Just remember, your aim is to light up and brighten lives, so steer off sarcasm, cynicism and scepticism, as these approaches might hurt someone or tarnish the atmosphere between you.

Coming up with a good-hearted joke feels brilliant in itself; the laughter you create is the delicious icing on the cake.

Today's thought

BUBBLES
A goodhearted quip has more bubbles of happiness than a glass of champagne.

Instant happy

WEAR MAD HATS
Why not raise money
for your pet charity
by getting all your
co-workers to be
sponsored to wear a
mad hat when they go
out at lunchtime?

Do something quixotically off the wall. Dream up something that's wild and wonderful, as long as it doesn't hurt anyone else, of course. Have fun seeing if you can get it to happen.

Even if it turns out not to lead anywhere, you will have created a wonderful flight of fancy, giving others huge pleasure along the way. Best of all, if it's something deeply honorable and chivalrous, something to benefit your favorite charity, perhaps, or to take a friend's mind off the hard times she's been having, so much the better. Go on, set your imagination free and come up with a gloriously fun idea.

Let each other grow

All the time you're growing and maturing, you're finding out about yourself and learning about life, too. And so is everyone else in your life, including your nearest and dearest.

The more aware you are of this on-going process and the more you acknowledge and review it, the easier it is to accept each other's changes and let your love adjust in tandem. That way you can support each other's maturing process and help yourselves to be who you really are right now, in the best way possible. Help each other to grow and to be your true selves, and to shine with happiness, as you are meant to.

I'll let you grow. You'll let me grow. We'll learn from each other, and we can grow together.

Marianne Williamson

Hands are on show all day and they are always there. If you use them in your work, they are even more in your line of sight. So think of the potential for pleasure and happiness the way they look can give you.

Why not start looking after your hands by giving yourself regular manicures. Be experimental: try painting your nails crazy new colors. Who said that your nails had to look conventionally natural or plain-polished? Express your personality!

When you make serious mistakes in life, intentionally or inconsiderately doing something wrong, you need to be able to put it behind you afterwards.

The best plan is to follow this scheme: regret it, show your remorse to those affected and learn what you can from the experience. If possible, make some atonement to redress the damage done in some way. Then forgive yourself and leave it behind you. Beating yourself up won't help anyone. Retrieve your happiness and then move on.

Instant happy

YOUR STEP-BY-STEP PLAN
1. Regret it
2. Show remorse
3. Learn
4. Atone
5. Forgive yourself
6. Move on

Instant happy

A CAT ON YOUR LAP

While you are sitting still, maybe working or watching TV, let your cat sit on your lap. Enjoy his presence, love and purr.

For health and happiness combined, stroke a cat. The frequency of his purr will resonate with the healing power of your body. The sound is soothing and the happiness it signals is infectious.

His shape and coat also give pleasure to you; they feel gorgeous under your hands. The look of him, taking in the beautiful markings, the exquisite whiskers, tail and paws will all bring a smile to your lips. And the affection the two of you exchange is an extra, important pleasure. Enjoy!

Give thanks for water!

Be like a hippopotamus; love the water you wash in! Wallow in water and give your gratitude for it. Water is one of our most precious commodities. So instead of taking your constant supply of hot and cold for granted, give thanks for it every time you use it.

Delight in the feel of water against your skin, as though you've reached an oasis after months in the desert. Appreciating the blessing intensifies the pleasure it gives you. It's not just a little everyday luxury; it's a huge one.

Instant happy

WASHING THOUGHT

Whenever you wash your face or hands, as the water runs out of the tap and over you, take a moment to remember how important the gift of water is to us.

*D*o you ever catch yourself obsessing about an uncomfortable situation you can do nothing about? For example, it's pointless stressing about something going on in your neighborhood which doesn't involve you at all.

So halt your mind's incessant circling. Tell yourself firmly it's not necessary to address it now and change the subject of your thoughts to something that does need your attention. If there's nothing waiting, think about something special in your life or something inspiring and creative. You are what you think, so think positively and you'll feel positively happy.

Recall a flower's scent

Sink blissfully into the scent of a bunch of flowers, or just one single bloom. Delicious floral scent has the power to give you pleasure in the moment so intense that your brain records it in incredible detail. The detail is so precise that your brain can recall it at will.

Think of smelling a heavily scented rose. Concentrate on it. There, isn't it gorgeous, right now? Lily of the valley does it for many people, too. What about you? What's the scent you most love and can easily recall? Indulge and feel real joy.

Families are a great source of happiness, but don't their problems cause you a lot of worry, too? It's hard to avoid this because you love them and are bound to feel concerned about them. But don't let their down times spoil your general outlook on life.

Instead, take an overview, remembering that life is something of a helter-skelter for all of us. Just as you ride the ups and downs, so will they. You can't wave a magic wand to make everything all right for them. But you can bless their lives with your love and emotional support and that will mean the world to them. Remember this and be glad that you are there for them. Your support gives them happiness, too.

Listen to choral music

The beauty and emotion of choral music is moving and joyous. It gives you a high as you listen and it enriches your life. Choose something that resonates with the spiritual part of your mind. You'll feel lifted to a higher plane of consciousness.

Go the extra mile

Increase your satisfaction and fulfillment in your work by going, if not always an extra mile, a little bit further than you absolutely need to. This doesn't mean working overtime, it's about doing your best. Your work will benefit and you'll reap another reward; pride in a job well done.

Whether you are busy or relaxed, enjoy watching the world go by. The expressions on people's faces are fascinating and so is the way they move, their body language and, young or old, their intrinsic beauty. Don't stare or you'll make people self-conscious and they'll think you rude; just quietly notice. This is a way of engaging with your fellow human beings.

You'll be astonished how interesting each person is and what you learn about them just from paying attention to them. It can be very moving. It can make you look at yourself in a new light. It feels good.

here's nothing like working outside in the fresh air for blowing away a few cobwebs of melancholy. Gardening is a great way to do this. So tend your own garden, a friend's, your neighbor's, or perhaps you have an allotment that needs your attention.

Or maybe you could do some voluntary work in a conservation area. Digging, pruning, weeding and clearing are good for your circulation and warming you up; the extra oxygen this delivers to every part of your body and brain acts as a feel-good tonic. Planting is an expression of faith and hope in the future. Harvesting, whether in flowers blooming or vegetables maturing, is a different kind of joy, a celebration.

Instant happy

BRING THE OUTDOORS IN

When you are outside gardening, pick a few flowers or bits of greenery to place in a small vase on your desk; a reminder of nature to have with you indoors.

How did you do?

Whether you tried out several ideas this month or just one, you might like to reflect on what you chose to try and why, and if it worked for you.

1. How many activities did you try this month?

- 1–3 activities
- 4–10 activities
- 11–20 activities
- 21–30 activities

2. How many did you repeat several times in the month?

- 1–3 activities
- 4–10 activities
- 11–20 activities
- 21–30 activities

3. Which activities had a positive effect on your mood this month?

Use the page opposite to make notes about what worked for you and what didn't.

Notes, jottings and thoughts

Love your body

Think nice things about your body and you'll have a profound effect on your health and happiness. Research has shown that when someone looks at a glass of water positively and lovingly the tiny crystals that it's made of become beautifully shaped. Think ugly thoughts and, sure enough, the crystals assume ugliness.

Your body is much the same. Its cells, which are constantly renewing themselves, respond to your having a loving, happy attitude toward them. Feeling good toward your body creates contentment and has a positive effect on your whole wellbeing.

Dress not just because you have to clothe yourself, but because it's fun and gives you and others day-long pleasure. You could choose a whole outfit that you enjoy putting together and feel all-round good in. Or it could be one item of clothing that always makes you feel a million dollars.

Alternatively, simply choose an accessory that gives you a thrill of pleasure, like a scarf in a color that really suits you, fab shoes or an eye-catching piece of jewelry. Wearing something that lifts your spirits will make you feel good all day and give pleasure to others, too.

Let people help you

Instant happy

PRACTICE MAKES PERFECT

Make a point of saying 'yes please' whenever you get the opportunity.

It's so easy to be too self-sufficient or proud to accept offers of help from others. Just for a change, be generous to yourself and the person who's offering to help you by saying, 'Yes please, that would be brilliant.'

Most people love to be helpful and are often denied the chance. So you'll be helping them by letting them do something for you. It's wonderful to have help and it feels great to say 'thank you', too. So accept any offers of help gracefully. As well as assisting you, it will increase the friendship between the two of you.

Share someone else's joy

Rejoice with friends and their successes and happiness will make you happy, too. When something marvellous happens to a friend, it's natural enough to think, 'Oh I wish it could have been me', and envy, even jealousy, might easily follow.

Stop this feeling before it gains ground by switching your reaction to an open gladness for them. Say how pleased you are, enthusiastically. Give them a hug, dance around the room with them. Genuinely sharing in their joy like this, you'll feel so pleased you kicked the negativity and gave yourself over to the pleasure of seeing their pleasure. Soon, enthusiasm for others' successes will be second-nature and automatic and you'll really notice a personal feel-good factor.

It's important to exercise regularly, but start small. Begin with easily achievable goals you know you can reach and be pleased when you do. Remember that exercising frequently helps keep you enthusiastic, as does mixing relatively relaxed exercise, for example going for a walk, with something more demanding, such as a gym work-out.

Decide how often you can viably set aside the time and willingly and reliably keep to your plan. Rituals like putting on jogging clothes feel good and prepare you well.

Being fit increases your health and well-being, too. And it feels great while you're doing it, not to mention satisfying afterwards. Don't just think about it, get going!

Self-belief is vital for good luck. For example, believe you're a lucky person and then give yourself lots of opportunities to be lucky. For starters, you could try entering competitions. Ignore the expensive phone-in types, but instead go for free ones, or those that genuinely help a favorite charity. No promises that you'll win anything, of course, but hey, you might!

More importantly, thinking of yourself as a lucky person feels great and encourages sideways-thinking, opening you up to your full potential to succeed at whatever you do and also to come up with great ideas. Feeling lucky is to feel good about yourself. We all have ups and downs in life, but feeling lucky is a great way to go, and it increases your chances of success.

Today's thought

GOOD LUCK!
If you feel lucky, you'll be lucky.

day 68

Love the journey

It feels good to have goals and great to realize them. But the best bit of all is the journey that takes you toward them. The loving striving is a success and a victory in itself. Be aware of your enterprise, energy and courage and absorb happiness from the knowledge of it, every step of the way.

day 69

You are unique

Like a snowflake, you are unique. No one else in the whole world is the same as you. Even if you are an identical twin, your soul is always your own, your thoughts and moods yours to forge, your willpower yours to use. Wonder at this astonishing fact. Special? You bet!

Time expands to fit the friends available. So give new friendship a chance to flourish by being open, warm and friendly to all you meet.

You've got a good circle of friends already? Fine, but there's always room to add another. Friendships vary and needn't necessarily be full-on, time-consuming ones. Stretching out a hand of friendship to someone you like, or who indicates that they like you, always feels good. So what if a bond doesn't form between you after all? Getting to know someone, even a little more, and giving friendship a chance to flourish feels good, even if it doesn't lead anywhere. And who knows? You may forge a strong friendship. Great!

Revive your childhood love of sparkly, eye-catching things. Just as they fascinated and delighted you then, they still can now, if you let them. As we grow older other people, fashion and us ourselves begin to impose all kinds of constraints and checks on what's cool and what isn't. That's fine, to an extent, if you enjoy being conventional and stylish in the current vogue. But you'll be surprised how good it feels to revel in at least a few pretty or shiny or brightly colored things. And they'll remind you to lighten up, too.

Remember how thrilling sparklers and all kinds of other sparkly things used to be? Enjoy them every bit as much now; the pleasure's childlike, not childish, and a splendid, shiny bit of happiness at any age.

The most unlikely friendships can develop if you are thrown together accidentally. So give affection a chance. Perhaps, for example, you are ill-assorted relatives, neighbors, colleagues or fellow committee members. Instead of gritting your teeth and assuming you've got nothing in common, amicably decide to get on with each other, one way or another. The relationship that develops can be surprisingly enjoyable, and a particular bond may well develop that is very precious to you. It can of course, perhaps it always does if we recognize it, develop into love.

So give a relationship with someone you have little in common with a chance to blossom by rubbing happily along together.

> Affection can rub along with the most unpromising people. Its especial glory is that it can unite those who most emphatically, even comically, are not made for each other.
>
> C S Lewis

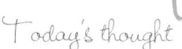

Today's thought

THINK ABOUT SUCCESS

Remember: the greatest and only reliably pleasing success is to be a kind, considerate and loving person.

Sure, the success of earning money and building and maintaining a comfortable lifestyle can be immensely satisfying. But it's only deeply satisfying if you couple it with the greater personal success of being a kind, just and likeable person.

If you do this you'll have the abiding pleasure of loving others and of being much loved and valued in return, for the best possible reasons.

Have you ever thought of getting your ideas flowing by starting an inspiration scrapbook of images and words that you love?

Use this book for whatever you like. It could be to record events in your life, or to help inspire you with future creative projects. Collect cuttings, scraps, snippets and stick them in. Arrange them artistically and take pleasure in doing it.

Add your own pieces of writing, letters, postcards, pressed flowers and leaves, theatre tickets and invitations. You could also include pieces of ribbon, colorful braid and stickers. These could be all decorated in your own style with colorful artwork. Stick in images, sayings, poems, quotes; anything that pleases or inspires you or makes you think 'Yes, that's so true!'

Howerver healthily you usually eat, sometimes there's nothing like some 'comfort' food to pep you up. When you can do with some soothing and cushioning from life's rough and tumble, what you fancy comes up trumps.

Choose comfort food carefully and it will make you feel better and be deliciously satisfying. Prevent a 'wish-I-hadn't-eaten-that' aftermath by choosing a snack or meal that you will really, really, love. Don't ever eat any old carbs just because they're there. And do relish the food; don't shove it down as quickly as you can, but linger over it and love every mouthful.

Don't put yourself down

Do you ever put yourself down, give yourself bad PR, even just in jest? Well, try not to as it's not good for you. You need to get into a more positive mode. So, from today, don't allow yourself to be self-deprecating. You may think it's harmless enough, but other people, and your own subconscious, will believe any bad publicity you put out.

So cut out negative statements like 'I can't draw' or 'I'm hopeless at maths', or worse. You hear so many people saying 'I'm useless', when most of the time it isn't true. Take an upbeat approach like 'I'm learning and it's exciting', or 'I'm good with money some of the time'. You are hugely capable when you put your mind to it and recognizing and believing in your ability feels great.

Today's thought

FROM TODAY
No more self-deprecation.

85

day **77** | Be firm

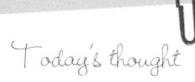
Today's thought

JUST SAY 'NO'
When you mean 'no', just say it!

Value yourself, at all times. Your time and your happiness can all too easily be nibbled away if you keep bending and swaying to friends' demands. It's a sad fact that the nicest of people can become surprisingly persistent pesterers. Don't be coerced by the pressure they put on you. When you definitely don't want to do something and, after due reflection, still don't want to, stick to your guns. A phrase they'll almost certainly back off from is 'That sounds like emotional blackmail to me!'

The other tactic, of course, though we often forget to use it is to just say 'No'. You'll feel great if you stand your ground.

What is happiness like?

ow would happiness feel to you if it had a physical expression in your body? Take a few spare moments to think where and how it would manifest itself.

Is your happiness internal, in your diaphragm, stomach or heart? Does it make you walk in a different way? Is it a tingle in your skin, as though you've been brushed by an angel's wing? It might be like the taste of honey in your mouth or maybe your shoulders feel relaxed when you're happy. Think about what it's like for you.

Today's thought

WHAT IS YOUR SPECIAL HAPPINESS-SENSATION? Recognizing your special physical happiness-sensation, you can relive it right now. This helps you to appreciate happiness whenever it's with you.

When trouble strikes, it's only natural to feel helpless, and even defeated. You can't see a way out of your difficulties and you are afraid that you'll be stuck in the problem for ever. But you know, you will get through this. Do what you can to resolve your difficulties; things will sort themselves out eventually and you will be happy again.

Repeating a time-honored quote to yourself, whenever your spirits flag, will renew your courage and optimism and open the door for troubles to move out and happiness to move back in.

A happy relationship isn't about hard work or a forced input of love and commitment. Its success comes from pooling resources willingly and, often, spontaneously. It's in giving that love grows and it takes two to make it work.

Appreciate all you can be to each other and all you have to give and share. Pulling together on this one is a form of happiness as sweet as honey, but never, ever cloying. Share your lives and love generously and you'll be sure to share happiness.

Today's thought

IT TAKES TWO
You know that well-worn phrase 'It takes two to tango.' Well, it's really true.

day **81**

Appreciate your ability

It's true, but it's all too easy to forget: gloating over or lusting after financial riches doesn't make you happy and it never will, but thinking about all the other ways in which you are rich does.

You are astoundingly rich in ability or wisdom and, depending on how much you use this ability, you can build and increase this wealth.

Whatever age you are you can take a warm, vibrant interest in others and enjoy hobbies, work and learning something new. Most of all, appreciating this amazing wealth gives you a deep feeling of abundance. Love your life with a passion! Be happy in its richness.

Sometimes you may need a little symbolic help to be happy. How about reminding yourself of your happiness by doing something concrete? You could try lighting up your happiness with candlelight. Surrounding yourself with candles, so that light and shadows play all around the room can be like gentle laughter.

There's something about candlelight that's mystical. Certainly it brings out a feeling of being at one with your own spirituality. And also it has a simplicity that creates a calm, blissfully simple, happiness. Enjoy the magical simplicity of candlelight.

WHAT ARE YOUR WAYS TO BE HAPPY?

Have a go at all the everyday ways to be happy in this book and add your own special ones, too. Help out your happiness gene and practice, practice, practice being happy!

Is there a 'happiness gene'? Apparently, the answer's 'yes'. But if you don't seem to have inherited one, no problem.

Like any emotional ability or tendency, it's perfectly possible to learn how to have a happy attitude, but you need to encourage and practice it so that it becomes as much second nature as if you were born with it already well-formed.

Try some useful mental imagery. 'Frame' a part of your life, to put the spotlight on its potential for happiness. Just as framing an already lovely picture makes it look even better and focuses attention on it, so does putting an imaginary frame around an aspect of your life that you rather like, but whose possibilities you've never much noticed, let alone maximized.

Now think sideways and look at it from all angles and directions, too. You'll immediately feel an excitement as your creativity is given room to breathe and fly. Opening yourself up to new ideas like this feels fantastic.

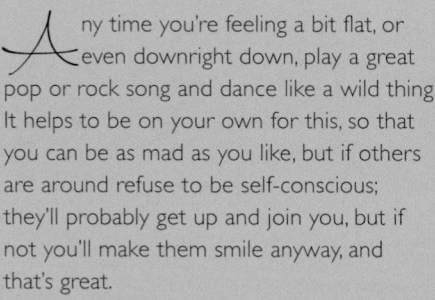

Any time you're feeling a bit flat, or even downright down, play a great pop or rock song and dance like a wild thing. It helps to be on your own for this, so that you can be as mad as you like, but if others are around refuse to be self-conscious; they'll probably get up and join you, but if not you'll make them smile anyway, and that's great.

The beat, the melody, the frenetic activity all work together to raise your heartbeat, get your circulation flowing better and all those feel-good chemicals whizzing through you, too. Dance! The high you get is happier, and a whole lot healthier, than any mood-altering drug, and it's long-lasting, too.

Stop before you've had too much and you'll defy the maxim that nothing lasts for ever.

Resist the temptation to keep on and on indulging in something delicious, be it food, sex, a hobby, or anything else that you simply cannot resist, and you won't run the risk of the good time going stale on you.

That way you'll leave it while you're still thoroughly enjoying it, and so be able to come back to it another time and enjoy it to the full all over again. And you'll have both the memory and the anticipation merged together in between. Brilliant!

Ever wondered about the value of 'micro-managing'? This is where you feel you want to control every single detail of your life and often other people's, too. Frankly, just thinking about it is exhausting, isn't it? So how about just loving yourself and your loved ones and letting everything else just happen as it happens to happen.

The first time out, pick a day when there's nothing terribly important going on! But even on workdays, and if you have kids, in term-time, you'll be surprised how everyone's world progresses through the day. As long as you've shaken off that 'must do this feeling', you'll notice how great it feels not to micro-manage, and how some really nice things happen all by themselves.

> Try just letting things happen from time to time. The world is full of delight if we just allow it to tell its own story without our interference.
>
> Leo E Buscaglia

Enjoy your own company

It's nice to be alone sometimes isn't it? You may have forgotten how good a little solitude feels and how important it is, too. So make and take advantage of opportunities a little quiet. Set out to enjoy your own company and you'll discover being on your own can actually feel very companionable and comfortable. It's also valuable you-time to reflect, relax and recharge.

Enjoy reviewing where you are in your life right now and, if you like, future dreams and plans. Or simply enjoy the peace and quiet. Either way, being alone feels wonderful and replenishes your zest for life.

I t's all too tempting to sit there complaining about something and blaming it on someone else. So don't just grumble on about what's wrong with, for example, TV or politics; do something about it today.

Write to the producers or the politicians involved or to the letters' page editor of your local or national newspaper and express your feelings and opinions. Being proactive in this way feels really good; it gets the frustration out of your system and, who knows, may even get a result. Yes!

Sitting wondering what to do, or putting off all the things you need to do, can hold back your happiness. Getting going on something instantly gives you a feeling of connection and involvement. If it's something you need to do you'll feel pleased with yourself that it's underway and probably end up enjoying doing it far more than you thought.

Happiness arrives with most forms of activity: work, play and any kind of creativity. When you're really into something there's a feeling of being in the flow; you hardly realize that time is passing and you feel fully engaged. Afterwards you'll feel pleased with yourself and well satisfied.

The brain needs exercising, just like your body does. So give your brain a regular work-out with a mind-stretching exercise that appeals to you. For example try a sudoku puzzle or a crossword.

Having a go at it, whether you are a beginner or an expert, is pleasantly challenging. Practicing gets your brain working well and, surprisingly perhaps, the concentration is extremely relaxing. It always feels good to know you've tried, even if you don't quite manage to work it out this time. If you do, of course, you get a big splash of satisfaction! You'll give your happiness muscles a work-out too.

Shall I do this or shall I do that? Do you ever put off making a decision and flit from one possibility to another in your mind? And have you noticed that if you never settle on any one route, it leaves you feeling unsettled and grumpy?

When that happens you need to bite the bullet and make a decision right now. Just do it! Once you get down to it you realize it isn't so bad after all, and don't you feel great afterwards? Your happiness is restored because you have cut the procrastination and got on with the job. Yes!

How did you do?

Whether you tried out several ideas this month or just one, you might like to reflect on what you chose to try and why, and if it worked for you.

1. How many activities did you try this month?

- 1–3 activities ☐
- 4–10 activities ☐
- 11–20 activities ☐
- 21–31 activities ☐

2. How many did you repeat several times in the month?

- 1–3 activities ☐
- 4–10 activities ☐
- 11–20 activities ☐
- 21–31 activities ☐

3. Which activities had a positive effect on your mood this month?

Use the page opposite to make notes about what worked for you and what didn't.

Notes, jottings and thoughts

I'm most content and happy when I have a strong yoga practice. It develops a wonderful feeling of stillness inside.

Gillian Anderson

Try a little yoga; it's a wonderful practice. You can carry out practical asanas and exercises with the intention of tuning in to the universal spirit, or you can simply do them to relax. Either way, they are incredibly calming and in the stillness or gentle movement come peace and a quiet contentment and happiness.

Yoga is good for your body and posture, too, and you'll take the poise and confidence it gives you, physically and emotionally, into the rest of your life. You can do yoga alone or in a group; you can be self-taught or learn from a teacher. You will achieve instant and enduring happiness and balance in your life.

For a guaranteed daily happiness, sprout seeds. Did you grow mustard and cress as a kid? Wasn't it a little bit of magic, seeing those seeds split and send out shoots, watching them grow, and then tasting their unique spiciness?

Why leave this experience to children? It's a brilliant thing for you to do as an adult now. The fun's the same and you can sprout all kinds of seeds and beans for the different nutrients and tastes they're bursting with.

Set a new batch of seeds to sprout every few days and you'll have a continuous supply of a true wonder food plus all the fun of watching it grow.

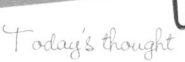

Today's thought

NOTICE CLOUDS
Just for today, look at clouds. Observe what kind they are. Name them if you can. Otherwise just see whether they are fluffy, wispy, billowing or streaky.

*L*ook up, rather than down, raising your chin and eyes, and experience the sudden rush of happiness it brings.

You could look at the tops of buildings, the sky above or the hills around you, if you are lucky enough to have them, or even just at the ceiling.

The act of angling your head upward and raising your eyes causes a physiological response. You feel lighter and brighter. Of course, if the view happens to be beautiful, it gives an added sense of joy!

Exercise aerobically

Re-energize your circulation and happiness simultaneously by trying some aerobic exercise. You'll find that it helps to give your spirits an incredible uplift.

Even a gentle form of exercise, such as walking, is good. Increase your speed very gradually so you don't jolt or jar your muscles or strain any part of you.

The aim is to increase your oxygen intake as you build speed and breathe faster and deeper. Don't overdo it and do enjoy the gentle slowing-down process; it feels fantastic as your circulation pumps feel-good chemicals around you body. Afterwards you'll continue to glow for ages.

Instant happy

DANCE WITH A CHILD

Just for fun, dance with a child today. This could be your own child, or a friend or relative. You'll give such delight and joy and children love seeing grown-ups being light-hearted and frivolous.

Dance across the years by dancing the way you and your friends did when you were teenagers. You might find yourselves dancing through the generations with the Charleston, a waltz, the Twist, the Jive, the Ceroc or a salsa!

Learning something new, the different rhythms and the laughter as you get it wrong all conspire to make you feel great. And then there's the bliss of old memories flooding back in. Have a mad, fun time dancing with the whole family.

The next time there's a clear sky at night, go outside and gaze up at it. Feel the awe of its beauty and infinity. See how many constellations you can identify. If you don't know their names, have fun seeing pictures or patterns in clusters of stars and give them your own names.

Let this activity spark an ongoing interest in the zodiac and astronomy. Who knows, one day soon you may even get to take a trip into space and maybe, within your lifetime, another life-supporting planet will be discovered. Let the mystery and beauty put your life into perspective and let happiness at being a part of our amazing universe flood through you.

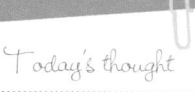

day 99 *Befriend your appetite*

Today's thought

LISTEN TO YOUR BODY
Today, eat only when you're hungry. Don't worry about the clock.

Eat the way that's right for your body and your personal style. The best way to do this is to make friends with your appetite and listen to it carefully. Tune in to your energy needs and what's comfortable for your digestion, too.

Do you like one or two substantial meals a day, or do you prefer to graze on several smaller ones? Do you like to balance calorie intake and expenditure by totting them up as you go, or do you prefer simply to eat healthily, adjusting how much you eat if your clothes feel too tight or too loose? Getting in tune with what's right for you feels wonderful and all adds to a happier you.

See a door closed not as rejection but as a potential for something that will prove to be much better and more 'you'.

If a door is shut in your face, don't keep banging on it or sink into a heap of despair.

Get on with the rest of your life, relishing all that's good in it. Meanwhile, explore new avenues, people, possibilities. If you have faith in the idea, think how you can progress it through other doors and down other avenues. Or perhaps it's time to move on and work on something completely different for a change.

Instant happy

CHOOSE A HAPPY MANTRA
Onward and upward is a great mantra for happiness.

When a poem resonates with you, learn it by heart to keep the wonder of it at your fingertips. Read lots of poetry as eclectically as you like, taking in work that's new to you as well as already beloved classics.

When you feel yourself connecting with the sentiment of a poem, it's a truly uplifting moment. That's the one to learn!

Memorizing the words is satisfying in itself and it fixes the meaning of the poem in your mind, so you can relive the pleasure any time you like.

Mix with happy people

Mix as much as possible with upbeat, happy people. Quiet or exuberant, they'll all share a positive attitude and their cheerfulness will encourage yours. You'll feel good when you're with them and afterwards, too. You're bound to be affected by their happiness, so let it be inspirational.

Become a hugger

Hug more, hug often, hug with a heart full of love, compassion and empathy. Hug as a welcome or as a goodbye. Hug to share joy or sorrow. When you lose inhibitions that make you hold back from touching others, you feel freer, kinder and more expressive. Most of all, hug because it feels wonderful.

Tune in to your inner wisdom for a deeply contented feeling. Listen to the sound of your inner being. Take a few moments to chill out and listen. To what exactly? It's your choice as to how you think of it. You might like to say you're listening to your intuition, to your relaxation, to God, or to the universal spirit and energy that runs through our world.

Something that casts light on a problem or that inspires you in some way may come to mind. Or you may simply benefit from the moments of deep relaxation. It feels wonderful.

Take a spontaneous day off and make a trip to the seaside to admire the beauty of the coastline and waves. Revel in the invigorating beauty, fresh air and fun. Enjoy the wonderful scent and freshness of the sea air. Have fun paddling at the water's edge or going for a swim and enjoy the delicious sensation of your toes sinking into the sand.

Write your name in the sand or build a sandcastle. Then perhaps go for a walk or a run along the beach. Make a collection of sculptural bits of driftwood or sea glass. In summer enjoy all the carefree summer fun and in winter wrap up warm and be invigorated by the bracing air.

Instant happy

SEASIDE TREASURES

On your return home, place small found objects in a little bowl on your desk. Whenever you look at them, you'll be reminded of your spontaneous trip to the seaside.

day 106 — Think on your feet

Enjoy thinking on your feet as things change and you'll keep your happiness momentum going. When your life doesn't work out exactly as you'd like, take things in your stride and don't waste time and energy fretting about it.

Resisting and complaining just make you miserable and don't help at all. Think instead of the best way to adapt your plans and make the best of the adjusted situation. Along with ongoing willingness and enthusiasm your newfound spontaneity will transform the way you handle the ups and downs of the day.

ike a beautiful painting, you are a work in progress and you are also the artist of your life. So plan your picture lovingly every day. Paint it in colors you like and make it just the way you want it.

Love the work you do and love being the artist at the heart of your life. It often takes a lifetime to find and settle into a style that's exactly right, depicting the real you. As you change and mature, have fun with each newly emerging style. Enjoy the discoveries, inspirations and satisfactions along the way.

Instant happy

FLYING VISUALIZATION
Close your eyes and sit in a quiet spot. Go right inside yourself and 'become' a bird flying. Visualize all the details as accurately as you can. You'll feel liberated.

It sounds a little mad, but try imagining that you're an angel. How can you light up your life and other people's? What can you do to protect yourself from their, and your, criticism and from depression?

Like an angel, take yourself lightly, so that you can fly. Feel and spread happiness where you can. Shake off the heaviness of gloom and doom and let good cheer pick you up and carry you, light as a feather. This feels amazingly good.

Enjoy the age you are

Enjoy the age you are now, with all your heart and all your energy. That way you won't have a chance to regret getting older, because the time you're having right now will always feel the best time you've ever had.

Don't sabotage the opportunity to be happy by resenting the negatives. Look for and love the good things in your life. Every single day, any time of your life, is full of opportunities to enjoy yourself. Take them!

Instant happy

'I LOVE THE AGE I AM NOW'
Say 'I love being 20, 30, 60, 80…' and you'll find you really do.

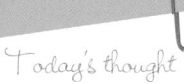

Today's thought

HOME PRESENT IDEAS

1. A bright new cushion.
2. A rearrangement of furniture.
3. A beautiful vase of flowers.
4. A new picture to hang on the wall.
5. A decorative pot that you found in a thrift shop.
6. A colorful sofa throw that you made.

Do something that will please your home and yourself. Give it a nice present today. You could simply spring-clean a little part of it with loving care. Or you could buy something that will really set off a room, giving yourself and others pleasure.

Homes respond to our joie de vivre and when you cherish yours, it will cherish you back. Feel this and bask in the warmth.

When someone is being troublesome or ratty, try to understand why they're behaving like this. This will help you not to take the negativity on board. You'll cope better and keep your equilibrium.

Perhaps you, given the same background and circumstances, would have acted in exactly the same way. Understanding enables you to forgive and to live lovingly, hopefully, kindly and inspiringly yourself.

You can't understand someone else until you walk in their shoes.

Anon

Instant happy

LAUGH AT YOURSELF

Laugh at yourself whenever you detect yourself being crotchety and self-righteous. In two shakes you'll feel relieved; your sense of perspective will be restored.

When somebody ruffles your feathers and you feel like squawking crossly, say to yourself: 'Do I look bothered?' It will make you laugh and defuse your anger.

Sometimes, of course, anger is justified. But when it's really not, laughing at yourself is the quickest way to stop being pompous.

As the anger fizzes out of sight, you'll think 'Ah, that's better.' Happiness, surprisingly often, is a matter of refusing to take yourself too seriously.

The happiness tip that most people mention first is to have a long soak in a lovely hot bath. And it certainly is a feel-good treat. The warmth, the silkiness of the water, the feeling of being cleansed, they all combine to give you a luxurious feeling of sheer pleasure.

Although even the simplest of hot baths feels great, by all means gild the lily by adding a few props to enhance the experience. Try candlelight, fragrant oils, a delicious drink or your favorite magazine.

'You're right; I'm wrong'

HOW DO YOU VIEW THINGS?

Today, try keeping an open mind. It will allow you to be a courageous, free and happy spirit.

Being relentlessly dogmatic can make you grumpy, not to mention those long-suffering souls around you. Discover the uplifting effect, to all concerned, by listening to other opinions, reviewing the facts and being brave enough to say, 'Hey, you're right, I got it wrong!'

Sometimes, of course, you will hold fast to an opinion. Just be prepared to look at the issue from all angles and make your mind up in the light of the new perspectives you suddenly see.

Collecting something that really appeals to you is an absorbing source of ongoing happiness.

Start a collection of things you love to look at and find interesting. There's something very beguiling about searching for and finding new pieces, and whenever you look through your collection you can relive the 'love of the chase'. You'll feel good all over again. And your satisfaction grows just like the collection.

Also, you can have a lot of fun getting to know other collectors. Many subjects have their own associations or clubs with regular meetings and talks.

Dress for happiness

Dress to feel good. Clothes express your personality, so enjoy trying to express the best aspects of yourself. Choosing clothes you love feels good in itself and also affirms that you feel good about yourself.

Dress for comfort, convenience, color, style, designer appeal; it's up to you. You might choose the same look every day or go for something completely different. The one golden rule is that whatever you put on, it must feel great.

Create a wonderful feeling of being in touch with someone you loved who has died by continuing to share the ups and downs of your life with them in your mind.

You can tell them what you think and figure out what they would say back to you. You can imagine phoning them to tell them of something great that's happened, or how relatives or mutual friends are doing.

Talking in your mind to loved ones who've passed on is a great way of keeping good memories of them alive and can be very comforting.

Learn something

When you're having a hard time, admit it and learn something from it, even though your spirits may have plummeted. Admitting to being upset helps recovery and the experience will highlight how wonderful it is to get back to everyday contentment and have some great times, too.

day **119** *Walk barefoot*

Why not walk barefoot? Around the house it can make you feel at home and happy. Outside there's a wholesome feeling of being in touch with nature. On grass or on the beach, it's a wonderful sensation. Feel the difference between soft, dry and firm, damp sand and notice how pleasurable it is.

Embrace the word 'yet'. It's easy to think you'll never fulfil this or that ambition or make a dream come true. And if you think like that, it's almost certain that nothing will happen. But if, instead, you say you haven't done it 'yet', you give possibility a chance. The suggestion that it could happen will encourage you to think sideways about how you can help it along.

Or, of course, if it's frankly nigh-on impossible, adding 'yet' will make you laugh. Either way, it's a feel-good word! When you say, 'My dream hasn't come true', add the word 'yet' and feel the tingle of pleasure.

*L*et your partner know that he counts. And enjoy the feeling that you count for him, too. It's easy in a relationship to get into the habit of leading such independent existences you hardly ever touch base, let alone express how important you both are to each other. But you know, doing so is vital to intimacy.

You don't have to make speeches, you can show your partner he matters to you in a thousand little ways. It's about tenderly recognizing his place in your life and valuing his presence there. It feels good to value each other, and show it.

Whatever your faith, visit old churches. It's said that where people have worshipped over many years the energy is very strong. Certainly, you'll probably sense, in many ancient places of prayer, a deep feeling of peace.

In addition, most churches are astonishingly beautiful, for the tiniest chapel and most magnificent cathedral were created with loving care. Enjoy the beauty, the sense of timelessness, the sense of being a witness to the eternal search for something 'other'. Look. Admire. Sit. Enjoy the peace. It's a timeless happiness.

Whether you tried out several ideas this month or just one, you might like to reflect on what you chose to try and why, and if it worked for you.

1. How many activities did you try this month?

- 1–3 activities ☐
- 4–10 activities ☐
- 11–20 activities ☐
- 21–30 activities ☐

2. How many did you repeat several times in the month?

- 1–3 activities ☐
- 4–10 activities ☐
- 11–20 activities ☐
- 21–30 activities ☐

3. Which activities had a positive effect on your mood this month?

Use the page opposite to make notes about what worked for you and what didn't.

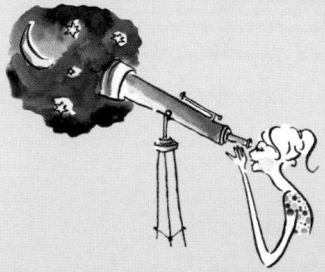

Notes, jottings and thoughts

SOME DESSERTS TO TRY
- Strawberry shortcake
- Pecan pie
- Banana split
- Brownies
- Cheesecake
- Fruit cobbler
- Pineapple upside-down cake
- Baked Alaska
- Bread pudding

If you feel like having a change, try a dessert after your main course; a sure route to a little happiness. A taste of sweetness finishes things off nicely and, in this day of one dish meals, is a treat to yourself and those you're cooking for.

It's a demonstration of your thoughtfulness to others and shows that you love to make that little bit of extra effort. Even people who say they don't like desserts will often have their special favorites.

A scrumptious dessert is a simple way to give yourself and your loved ones a little extra pure pleasure. Go the extra mile and serve a surprise dessert today.

Try out a new role

Feel stuck in a particular role? Why not re-jig it or take on a completely new one? This will help you to revive your happiness. For example, you could change places with someone else or even invent a completely new role for yourself.

This role could be in your local community, at the office or amongst friends. It could be anywhere where the familiar perception of you has become cloying or you no longer feel appreciated or even noticed.

Shake it up and play a different part. You'll show different aspects yourself and positively sparkle in the attention: both yours and theirs.

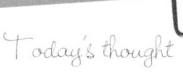

Today's thought

GRIEVE PROPERLY
Grieve as you need to.
It opens the door for
your happiness to come
back in.

If you have recently been bereaved, don't be afraid to mourn properly. When you've suffered a big loss, express your feelings. Although loss hurts, and is often excruciatingly painful, letting the emotion of sorrow flow is very comforting.

Being open about feelings takes less energy than suppressing them, so you won't get so exhausted. And when you've been bottling your feelings up, it's a huge relief to give in and grieve as you need to.

Have you ever tried out a treasure hunt? It's a fun activity, not just for kids, either. Why not join in one, or maybe even organize one yourself and enjoy the thrill of the chase.

If you want to plan and run your own treasure hunt, inventing clues and watching people work them out is both fun and highly satisfying.

Use your imagination, logic and map-reading skills to plot a route that's interesting and challenging. You'll be totally absorbed and thrill to the spirit of the puzzle-solving race.

Instant happy

RELEASE THE INNER POET!
If you can write poetry and are organizing the hunt, pen some clever rhyming clues.

Instant happy

CONSIDER YOUR ABILITIES

Are you practical, creative, emotional, academic, intellectual, intuitive, spiritual or scientific? Today, be thankful for whatever abilities you may have.

Now's the time to feel proud of your innate intelligence. Every time you say something like 'I'm thick', or 'I'm hopeless', you denigrate your true ability and chip away at your self-esteem.

You actually have an extremely complex brain, offering a wide span of different kinds of intelligence. You can improve the way it works in all respects if you've the will to.

Most important, though, is to recognize and maximize your particular talents. Do you have the knack of getting on well with people? Or are you practical, creative, emotional, academic, intellectual, intuitive, spiritual or scientific? Be glad about your own special abilities and use them as fully as you can.

Read a magazine

Sit down with a hot drink and your favorite magazine for a patch of pure pleasure. Go on, treat yourself! It's a good way of keeping up to date with a hobby or interest and it keeps you in the swing of the latest trends and fashions.

It feels companionable to be part of the magazine's readership and there's a pleasant sense of getting to know the regular writers, too. Reading articles and snippets about something you like, in an appealing style, is a recipe for enjoyment. Curl up with a magazine you love. It's pleasure guaranteed.

Instant happy

BE POSITIVE
Today, do whatever you've got to do with a positive attitude and you'll be surprised how much you enjoy yourself.

When you've got to do something that you don't want to, instead of dreading it and complaining about it, try doing it with good grace. Deciding to enjoy a task paves the way for doing just that. Take the view that it will only last for a short time in the context of your whole life, and will be well worth the effort.

A job well done equals deep satisfaction. Working towards that and enjoying the doing as well as the finishing feels really good and adds to your happiness.

Why not treat yourself to some cut flowers and then arrange them beautifully? If you've never experimented with flower-arranging before, you might be surprised at how creative it feels. A lovely flower arrangement, with the help of some greenery and florist's foam, is easy, creative and fun to make. You'll be amazed at how satisfying it is.

Put your arrangement somewhere prominent, where you'll see it a lot during your day. Look at it often and drink in the delight it gives you. A lovely arrangement is a great focal point for your home and happiness. Another idea is to create a pretty posy, using coordinating ribbons to secure it, and present it to a special person today.

Instant happy

WORK ON YOUR COLORS

Today, choose a favorite vase and select a range of flowers and foliage that accent the predominant colors. Or pick flowers that go with your home decor.

If you are suspicious about something negative, be alert to it, but beware of obsessing about it, possibly assuming the worst, when this isn't necessary.

Think about the cause and surrounding facts logically and let go of it if it seems unfounded. If not, deal with it appropriately but, again, let it go from your mind. If you're still uneasy, bounce it off someone who is sensible and well grounded and who will tell you if you're being paranoid.

Checking if your reaction to a suspicion is over-the-top frees you up to be soothingly logical and proactive, if necessary, and happy in yourself.

Happiness in nature

The mind-blowing beauty and perfection of the simplest meadow flowers transports you to heaven if you take a moment to look and be sent there by them. The joy is there for all of us, in all flowers and wildlife, always. Such treasure! Such happiness! How lucky we are.

Burn incense

Burn an incense stick and feel peacefully happy, maybe more in touch with the universe, too. Incense is often used in religions as an aid to prayer and to create a peaceful atmosphere. It may have aromatherapeutic qualities, and the ritual gives happiness in the moment.

When the weather's bad, you dress up warmly and cope with it as best you can. The same needs to happen when fate buffets you around emotionally. Go into survival mode and think how you can use prevailing circumstances the best way possible for yourself and any others affected.

Whether you take over the helm as leader or support someone else, relax and be happy in the knowledge that you're steering a good course through the elements. In a stormy setting, keep a calm mind and get a firm, sure picture of what's best to be done.

The wind blows east and the wind blows west, but it's the set of the sail, not the way of the gale that dictates the way you go.

Tennyson

Why not get into the habit of visiting someone elderly or housebound in your neighborhood every week? Having you pop in will brighten their day and they'll look forward to having your company for however long you can spare.

Seeing them regularly speeds up getting to know each other, allowing a pleasing camaraderie between you. Great for them and for you, too.

Be a buddy to someone who'll love your visits and enjoy the rapport that develops.

Today's thought

IF YOU NEED AN EXCUSE...

Don't be shy about visiting someone. But if you need an excuse, why not offer to do their shopping for them or tidy up their garden.

As long as you are basically happy with your gender, turn your acceptance into a positive enthusiasm. If you're a woman, for instance, be pleased about your femininity and positively enjoy it.

Whether you love being girly or like to highlight how female you are with a more 'masculine' style, let your self-assuredness shine through. Others will feel good in your presence and so will you.

Take off your watch

If you don't have any pressing appointments today, take off your watch and be 'time-free'. Enjoy a feeling of timelessness. When you are wearing a watch, you'll be inclined to clock-watch, monitoring how long you spend on things, and effectively curtailing your freedom.

Without a watch, time will run its course through your day as usual, but you can respond to it naturally. You'll eat when you're hungry, go out when you want to, spend as long on something as you wish to, and finally go to bed when you're tired. Brilliant!

Happiness can come free and unexpectedly — don't seek it too desperately. Relax and it will appear.

David Baird

ppreciate and love your body as much as you can. Don't do this in a narcissistic way. Do it for the sheer wonder and admiration of it. Isn't your body the most incredible construction? It's a complex and ingenious housing for you and every nano-cell has its rightful place and function.

Give thanks for your body, for every tiny bit of you, and take good care of it. Along with your mind and soul it's your most precious asset and a treasure trove of pleasures, too. Never cease to be astonished at, and thankful for, its extraordinary complexity and brilliant design.

o you remember going on nature rambles when you were a kid and making collections of leaves and other fallen things? Maybe you had fun arranging and displaying them when you got home.

Why not try and recreate this feeling? Like a child on a parkland or country walk, gather anything on the ground that you like the look of. This could include fir cones, an interesting piece of wood, a beautiful pebble, acorns, twigs and leaves.

When you get home, maybe make a box picture or mobile with them or display them in an appealing way. It will remind you of the pleasure of the walk and be a unique artwork to enjoy, too.

Instant happy

NATURE JOURNAL
When it comes to nature, don't forget your journal. Press leaves and flowers you collect and stick them in your journal.

149

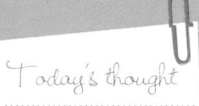

Today's thought

TAKE ITEMS TO A THRIFT STORE

If you don't like some of your clothes, perhaps there is someone else who will. And the money raised can benefit a charity, too. Doesn't that make you feel fantastic?

Spend time clearing out your wardrobe. Give away anything you haven't worn for a couple of years, or less than that if you know in your heart that you never will. Maybe you bought the item on impulse or perhaps it was on sale and seemed a good bargain. Eventually you realized you'd made a mistake.

It's better to have a few things you love and feel good in rather than loads of things you never wear. This process will highlight any additions that you really do need to make to your wardrobe. You'll feel organized and stylish and the feeling of being uncluttered, clotheswise, is liberating.

Sorting out your wardrobe makes you think about whether your clothes are really all working for their place there.

Conversation's great when it's not shark-infested and everyone will feel so much happier. So resist the temptation to make bitchy or cutting comments and don't accept them from other people either. If you feel any untoward comments about to slip out of your mouth, shut the door on them.

Stop unpleasant words before they have a chance to escape. Realize how mean you'll sound. And stop others' mean remarks by blanking them immediately. You didn't hear that, did you? You must surely have misheard; they surely wouldn't have wanted to hurt you…would they?

151

Have a go at baking some bread. You'll find it's pure happiness. Everything about making bread is feel-good, literally and emotionally, and it's surprisingly easy and quick to do.

Assembling the ingredients and getting the tins ready is settling and pleasantly anticipatory. Kneading the dough is deliciously sensual, and with a little practice it's pleasing to notice the unique feel when the gluten develops and it's proving time. A slow, cool rise slows down your pace, too, while a quick rise is exciting to witness.

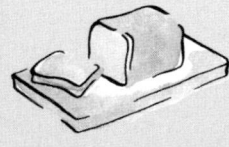

Being focused on what you want to do, for example in your career, is difficult if you're confused about what the options are. Instead of going round and round in circles, try focusing instead on what you don't want to do.

How to plan your life and go forward positively and happily again will suddenly become a whole lot more obvious and straightforward.

Do you remember how good ice cream was when you were small? It surely made you feel really happy. Now's the time to re-appreciate how wonderful it is, even though you're all grown up. Take your mind back to your then-favorite flavor and taste it all over again.

Maybe you loved ice-cream cones on the beach or a thick slab sandwiched between wafers. Now recreate the experience and enjoy ice cream with childlike enthusiasm and joy. Whatever your age, you'll feel young and happy.

Praise yourself

Use praise and encouragement to guide yourself forward. Stop all stern self-admonishments and harsh self-criticisms. Say to yourself, 'Come on, I can do this!' or 'Courage, I'm strong and capable.'

Use praise not to let yourself off the hook of effort, but to help yourself get back on course. Stay on it and get where you want to go. Use plenty of carrots of praise and encouragement rather than sticks of disapproval to beat yourself with.

Today's thought

ENCOURAGE YOURSELF!
Be who you want to be and go where you want to go.

Sometimes the saddest music is also the most joyous. Why not try listening to some achingly sad, hauntingly beautiful music. It could be blues, pop, folk or classical; whatever appeals to you in the moment.

Melancholy music will connect you with how it feels to have a heart that aches with sadness, and at the same time, with the joy of the love, deep inside you.

At the heart of the blues is not melancholy, but a strange and worldly joy.

Ian McEwan

A favorite chair is a great place in which to relax and put the world to rights. So choose a chair you really like and designate it as your own special one. Perhaps you could enjoy it for its comfort or perhaps more for its stylish lines or antiquity. Or perhaps the chair means a lot to you for some reason. Maybe it was your father's or mother's chair, for instance.

Throughout your life you may well spend quite a bit of time being at home and enjoying a beloved chair will make it all the more fulfilling.

Today's thought

MAKE IT YOURS
To really make your chair your own, leave your possessions, such as a book, letters, magazine, old sweater or knitting, on it.

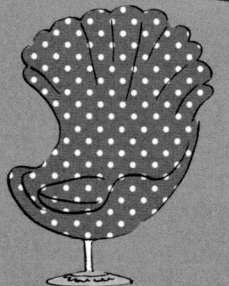

day 148 | Welcome the new day

Every morning when you wake up welcome the new day warmly. Showing your appreciation affirms your sense of being part of the world and you start off the day feeling glad and connected. The confidence and contentment this gives you make a firm foundation for a good day.

day 149 | Say 'I love you'

Say 'I love you' often. Say it to your partner, your parents, children, siblings, relatives, friends and pets. Say it to anyone you're fond of, too. The saddest thing is when someone dies and we wish we'd told them we loved them. The happiest thing is telling them: often, often, often.

Enjoy being happy

Being happy is a joy and however you get there, it's important to savor its reality. It's become fashionable among some scientists and journalists to infer that if happiness is created by the genes, a neurosis or a hormonal reaction, this devalues it somehow. But it doesn't, one iota.

Truth is, happiness, in any of its forms, is happiness and it's good to be happy, however we get there. Let's hope they read this book and catch the happiness bug!

If you like chocolate, treat yourself to an enjoyable amount, plenty enough, that is, but not too much, and luxuriate in the happiness it brings you. Indulge your passion for it. A not-too-big, not-too-small amount is all about the wonderful taste and also being nice to yourself. In addition to all that pleasure it contains natural feel-good chemicals like those associated with falling in love. These enhance endorphin levels, making you feel better still.

For a true taste of heaven on Earth, have a relaxing massage. If your partner offers to do the honors, make sure they realize it's not a prelude to lovemaking; that way you can lose yourself in sensation for its own sake.

Why not choose a specific area to focus the massage on, rather than going for an all-over? You may wish your masseur to concentrate on, say, your back, shoulders and neck, or to give you a luxuriously dedicated foot massage. Enjoy the total bliss that will come to you.

Instant happy

INDIAN HEAD MASSAGE
For a real Eastern treat, try out an authentic Indian Head Massage.

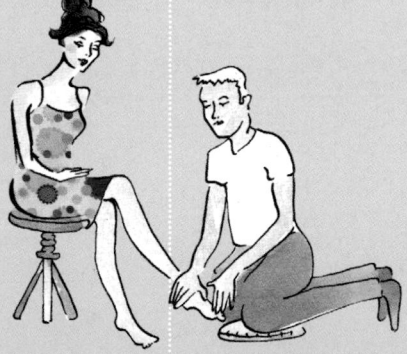

Whether you tried out several ideas this month or just one, you might like to reflect on what you chose to try and why, and if it worked for you.

1. How many activities did you try this month?

- 1–3 activities
- 4–10 activities
- 11–20 activities
- 21–30 activities

2. How many did you repeat several times in the month?

- 1–3 activities
- 4–10 activities
- 11–20 activities
- 21–30 activities

3. Which activities had a positive effect on your mood this month?

Use the page opposite to make notes about what worked for you and what didn't.

Notes, jottings and thoughts

Every day, spend a few moments being still, because in the stillness you can touch base with your soul. You could think of it as your inner being, the true 'you' deep inside your public image, or a dimension that is not yet fully explained.

In the stillness you will feel 'and hug to yourself' this intrinsic part of you, protect and love it and be protected and loved by it. This is the core of inner poise and contentment.

It's a common belief that we don't have enough free time to do the things we really want to do. Maybe there are lots of things you would like to do. Perhaps you would like to read more or pursue a neglected hobby, for example?

What you have to do is carve out the time; create it from the existing material of each day's twenty-four hours. Just think, if you set your alarm for an hour earlier each day, for example, watched less TV, or used the computer less, you could accumulate lots of extra 'you time'.

Today's thought

DO WHAT YOU WANT TO DO

Happiness is having time to do something you really want to do and having it in your control.

It's important to have a vision, a dream and to dare to dream. The good and the wonderful often starts with a dream.

Martin Luther King made a magnificent speech about tolerance and democracy, and his words live on, inspiring each generation as it comes along. Some 40 years on his dream is coming true. Courage and hope is there for all of us.

I have a dream.

Martin Luther King

At the summit of a hill or a mountain, you'll feel on top of the world and it's a wonderful feeling. There's something fantastic about reaching the top. It feels like a real achievement.

Whether you made it there on your own two feet or by other means, you'll feel pleased with yourself. And as you gaze at the view and soak up the panorama and the beauty, you'll feel truly wonderful. Up high like that you feel close to the sky and to heaven, too.

Instant happy

CHOOSE YOUR FAVORITES

When you are visiting a gallery, take extra time to select which artist and which paintings you like the best. Record your views and thoughts in your journal.

Looking at art, whether you prefer paintings or sculpture, can have a profoundly uplifting effect on you. The next time you get a free moment, visit an art gallery and take time to enjoy looking at the work there.

It doesn't matter whether the gallery is local or national, showing high-quality amateur work or contemporary or classic masterpieces by famous artists. See which pictures or sculptures resonate with you most, making you tingle with joy. Just remembering them will always vividly recall the pleasure you had today.

Sing out your joy!

Singing is a much-forgotten and ignored activity. People often assume that they 'can't' sing and won't even give it a go. But singing can be so good for you. Try singing solo in the bath or shower, in the countryside, your garden or a park, or sing with like-minded people, perhaps in a choir. As well as being an expression of your spiritual side, song can feel like a direct connection to the spirit. Let your delight in the world soar to the heavens.

Do you normally regard boredom as being a negative thing; something that you should avoid? Well, have a rethink. Perhaps you could actually use boredom as a launching pad for new interest and zest in your life. If you feel bored and unenthusiastic with things the way they are at the moment, terrific! Boredom is a wake-up call and a fantastic opportunity. It's a chance to realize what you need to do in your life, or to think about what you really want to do.

Nudged by boredom, fill your life with love and thought for another enjoyable activity, curiosity about our astonishing world and, last but not least, daydreams. Your life will be full of interest and happiness.

Shake hands

Think about the meaning of shaking hands. Every handshake is, potentially, a moment of welcome and fresh connection and every opportunity for a hand shake is to be enjoyed.

Why not shake hands voluntarily with all sorts of people you meet. Kids love it because it makes them feel special and mature, and adults like it, too, for much the same reasons. As part of our culture, the gesture feels pleasantly familiar and safe.

Today's thought

HANDSHAKE STYLE
Make sure your handshake feels good to others. Your clasp should be firm but gentle.

Today's thought

SPECIAL MUSIC
Have a lovely time choosing your own Desert Island Discs and thinking why each selection means so much to you.

Pretend you've been asked to appear on a program where people choose their favorite pieces of music and talk about why they're important to them.

Have fun playing the music you love most and which means most to you. Choose your final selection for the 'show'; it is sure to have huge emotional resonance with you as well as being musically enjoyable. Why do these pieces appeal to you so much? Perhaps they tell the story of your life. Enjoy the emotional journey this takes you on. Wonderful stuff!

Accept inevitability

Whatever happens in your life, it's a certainty that, come what may, you'll progress through it from start to finish. Accepting the inevitability of this frees you to make the best of every single day. You'll keep walking through the sad or bad times and fly with wings of golden light in good periods.

Be loyal

Loyalty is a virtue to be valued highly. So try to be as loyal as you can. It feels good to support and stand firmly by friends and colleagues. In helping build others' confidence, you'll build your own. You'll help them be and do the best they can. Loyalty feels good for everyone.

Feel the happiness of the company of other people and of crowds. In times gone by, people stuck together and were rarely alone; safety in numbers was key to their survival.

Today, happily, we are able to relax in solitude. But there is still something wonderfully comforting about being part of a group or crowd. So instead of withdrawing into your shell next time you're sandwiched between others, say on a bus or train, feel the joy of being in a crowd. Bask in its visceral and emotional comfort.

In former centuries, making pilgrimages was an activity that many took part in, to seek spiritual and religious sustenance. These days pilgrimage is far less common, but it is still considered a wonderful way to seek peace, connection and healing.

If this appeals to you, your pilgrimage could be something ambitious and challenging, like walking the Camino Way in Spain. If that's your dream, start planning now and, step by step, enjoy reaching your destination. But more local pilgrimages also give you the chance for a sacred quest. Visiting holy places like a saint's shrine or ancient standing stones, the feeling of connection and awe will heal and uplift you, filling you with a quiet but deep joy.

*M*editation refreshes you. Very simply, it's all about being still, both physically and in your mind. It's as though your soul has been gently washed in pure spring water, blessed by love. Try to learn to love meditating. If you are a beginner, books or a class will help to get you started on learning the technique.

Once you have got used to the practice, you may like to try listening for inner guidance or enlightenment. With a little practice, as meditation becomes a familiar pastime, you will relax more and more deeply.

hink of your bed as your nest, your safe haven and your supreme resting place. It's also the sexual base, if you've a partner, for your relationship. In all its different aspects, your bed needs to be deliciously inviting and if it looks appealing, it can be an oasis you can depend on for a happy rest overnight or any sojourn there during the day.

So, be sure to keep your bed looking fresh and inviting and you'll enjoy its welcome each night and maybe sometimes during the day, too.

Be honest about yourself in your work and life away from home and also be truthful to yourself and to your loved ones in your private life. Giving a false image is hard work to maintain and is sure to feel false to you, too.

How much better to let everyone know the real you and to be aware that you are genuinely loved, warts and all, for the person that you really are. It feels good, and it is far easier to be truthful about who you really are. You'll feel more relaxed and happy.

At night, assert your right to peace and sleep. Imagine taking all the niggles and fears of your day and popping them into a deep jar. Watch them tumbling to the bottom and screw on the lid.

Then place the jar on the floor. If you need to deal with any problems or issues in the morning, plan to do it then. For now, it's time to rest, peacefully and happily.

Today's thought

TONIGHT
Close down frets and fancies for the night and, with mind cleared and happiness given space again, you'll relax deeply.

It's great to share each other's day because it bonds you together and adds interest to your relationship. So be sure to light up tales of your day with interesting details you noticed and the way you felt about them.

Make a point of noticing fascinating little things during the day, good stories, your feelings and use them to add vividness to your conversations when you get back home. Talking over your respective days with loved ones is a real shared pleasure. It keeps you in touch with each other's lives and feels very intimate.

Ensure you feel good about what you eat by choosing shops whose suppliers have high standards of care. For example, if you eat meat, try to buy only from free-range suppliers. If this choice means that meat is an occasional luxury, that's all to the good.

You wouldn't feel good about yourself if you knew that meat had come from an animal that had led a miserable life. If animals are treated with respect and care, you'll enjoy your food all the more.

Instant happy

WRAP UP WELL
Pretty wrapping adds an
extra bit of pleasure to
any gift for both the
recipient and the giver.

On impulse, send someone a present
today and, however tiny or
inexpensive, wrap it up nicely, or hand-
decorate the gift note you send with it.

You'll derive lots of pleasure in the choosing,
the wrapping, the decorating and the giving.
And so will the recipient, knowing not only
that you've thought of them, but have taken
the time to wrap your gift attractively, too.

Be aware of your gift for brightening other people's lives and rejoice in using it as often as possible, every day.

You have a great ability to improve the lives of others. Even the smallest of kindly gestures may have a huge impact you never knew you had. Perhaps you held out a helping hand when someone infirm or elderly couldn't reach something in the supermarket, for instance. Use this gift as much as possible. It will give you great happiness, too.

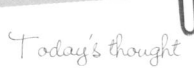

MANAGE YOUR AFFAIRS

It feels really good to manage your affairs well and this protects your happiness, too.

If you see trouble coming act quickly to prevent it actually taking shape and becoming a reality. So many problems and difficulties wouldn't actually come to fruition if we didn't bury our heads in the sand and took more notice of events outside ourselves.

Look ahead and be aware of what's going on in all aspects of your life. Have contingency plans ready in case you need to call on them, and be proactive.

Have a hot drink

There's nothing like a hot drink for soothing you when things go awry in your day. So when your equilibrium is disturbed, choose a favorite hot drink.

The ritual of making a drink and sharing it with others is soothing in itself. The warmth and the ingredients of the drink itself make you feel better, too. It provides a tiny oasis of happiness that can make all the difference in a troubled time. If you're cold and tired, have a luxurious hot drink. A steaming drink evokes a feeling of having been out in freezing weather and making it safe back to home and hearth. It's a great feeling.

Instant happy

HOT DRINK IDEAS
- Tea and coffee
- Cocoa and hot chocolate
- Fruit tea
- Soup
- Hot water with a slice of lemon
- Spicy mulled wine
- Apple juice

Look for the flip-side

Sometimes a failure can actually be a success, or at least the beginnings of one. Losing your job, for instance, is a chance for you to think about your direction in life. Or a broken relationship can open the door to future individual happiness for both of you. Even downright failure can transform into success if you learn from it and determine to handle things better in future. Taking a positive view of failure can be amazingly uplifting.

So looking for the flip-side of failure reveals the success and happiness potential, both today and in times ahead.

Words and behavior aren't always clear; sometimes you'll need to translate what you or others mean.

So if, even though you've listened carefully, you still don't understand someone, ask them to explain again. Repeat what you think they mean, for verification or clarification. And if someone's not getting what you're trying to say, try expressing it in a different way.

Today's thought

CLARITY
Understanding isn't always instant; a little clarification is often all that's needed for a relationship to run smoothly and happily.

Look lovingly

Look lovingly at your partner and others who mean a lot to you and enjoy it when the compliment's returned. One of the nicest things on this Earth is seeing the love-light in people's eyes as they look at you. Expressing your affection like this in your eyes feels pretty good, too.

Be sensitive

Be sensitive to others' feelings and take care not to press their buttons. Making others feel sore and threatened rebounds, for underneath we always know when we're mean and it feels unpleasant. Being tactful, soothing company makes you feel kind and happy.

Wrap up well and go for a walk in the rain with a friend or partner. During the walk and afterwards, you'll be glad you made the effort.

It feels wonderful to splash through puddles and even to feel the rain on your face. You'll be pleased with yourselves for braving the elements and the ridiculousness of choosing to do such a thing will make you laugh. You could, of course, sing and dance, too, if you feel carried away. It's great fun and it's wonderful, too, to get home, dry off and perhaps even reward yourselves with tea and cakes!

Daisies are our silver, buttercups our gold: this is all the treasure we can have or hold.

Jan Struther

Be positive about your relationship or friendships. The statement to yourself, or others, 'Yes I'm really happily married' or 'So-and-so is a very good friend of mine', encourages loyalty, affection, liking and, of course, love.

Such overt happiness creates a positive atmosphere around you that others will immediately sense and if they overhear your enthusiasm, they'll respond warmly, too. Believing in the happiness of your marriage or friendship is self-fulfilling.

$\mathcal{M}$aking a map or painting of your home or the area where you live is a great pastime and gives you a terrific sense of place and a buzz of happiness. Plus you'll have something nice to hang on the wall afterwards, especially if you have it framed. Try experimenting with different styles: your picture could be graphic, like a map, wildly impressionistic or even abstract.

You can include all the people you know in the neighborhood and any important landmarks. Your home is center-stage in your life, of course, so highlight it. It's fun and gives you a wonderful sense of familiarity and belonging.

Whether you tried out several ideas this month or just one, you might like to reflect on what you chose to try and why, and if it worked for you.

1. How many activities did you try this month?

- 1–3 activities ☐
- 4–10 activities ☐
- 11–20 activities ☐
- 21–30 activities ☐

2. How many did you repeat several times in the month?

- 1–3 activities ☐
- 4–10 activities ☐
- 11–20 activities ☐
- 21–30 activities ☐

3. Which activities had a positive effect on your mood this month?

Use the page opposite to make notes about what worked for you and what didn't.

Notes, jottings and thoughts

Give yourself carrots

Instant happy

IDEAS FOR 'CARROTS'

- Have a hot drink just the way you like it.
- Eat a piece of chocolate.
- Make a personal phone call, email or text.
- Go for a short walk.

I ncentives and little rewards, no matter how simple, can help to make your work pleasurable and successful. All in all, they are good recipes for a happy day.

So try giving yourself 'carrots' at various stages throughout your day. Promise yourself a coffee just the way you like it, for instance, when you've completed a section of your work. It will spur you on and give you a pleasing incentive. It will encourage you to concentrate, too, so your work will flow well and be more satisfying.

Rather than hoarding money and all the other good things in your life, let them flow on to other people. This then keeps the channels open for more supplies to come to you. This is one of the oldest wisdoms, and even more relevant in today's age of extremes of both abundance and poverty, than it's ever been.

So be as generous as you can with all that you have. More will come to you to pass on, and it feels right. Being generous is helpful to others and it feels wonderful for you, too.

Cast your bread upon the waters and it will come back as ham sandwiches.

Lee Cousins

There are plenty of tips in this book about giving yourself some tender loving care, but every now and then it's sheer bliss to lie, or sit, back and have someone else pamper you instead.

This could take the form of a day at a spa, luxuriating in the warmth of the pool and the surrounding leisure areas and having a relaxing treatment or two. Or maybe it could be a delicious meal at a favorite restaurant where you feel valued and superbly cared for.

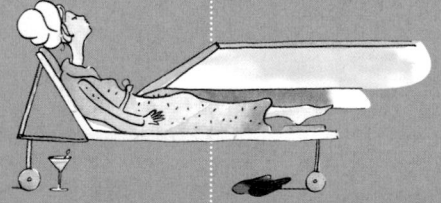

Be the controller of what happens to you in your life. Life is a mixture of colored threads intricately woven together to make amazing patterns.

Sometimes you are the weaver, but sometimes life dictates what happens and you just have to keep up, somehow, with the weft and waft of the loom. See yourself as a beautiful, rich tapestry and know that the work is good. All is well. Enjoy the idea that you and your life are weavers, together creating a rich tapestry of 'being' and 'happening'. Tingle with pleasure at this happy thought.

Instant happy

BE A MENTOR
When you mentor someone you see promise in, you'll mentor a good feeling about yourself, too.

Make someone else's progress your special project and become their mentor. This could be a young friend or relative who needs a guiding hand, or someone else who needs outside support.

Guiding and doing everything you can to give this person a helping hand along their path is as fulfilling for you as for them. The person will always remember your help and be glad of your assistance and proactive friendship. In turn, you'll feel a lasting glow of pleasure about what you did for them.

Take a dog for a walk

Why not take a dog for walk? If you don't have one of your own, borrow a friend's or offer to walk a dog in your neighborhood if the owner is too busy to do it.

Dogs adore going for walks and playing. They really delight in showing their pleasure and this pleasure is incredibly infectious; it will make you laugh, put a spring in your own step and maybe you'll feel like running and jumping for joy too! Share fully in the dog's abundant happiness.

How about organizing a 'favorite things' evening with friends? This could take a number of different forms. For example, you could each bring along a track of music you adore, a poem to read out or even a special anecdote to relate. It's important for everyone present to respect each others' choices and listen to each contribution with wholehearted attention.

You will find that because everyone is contributing different things, the variety on offer makes for a wonderfully eclectic mix.

Another, more light-hearted, idea is to bring unwanted clothes to swap, or take it in turns to experiment with makeup.

When someone pays you a compliment, make the effort to appreciate it fully. Show the person your full appreciation by actually beaming with pleasure, both inside and out.

A compliment is a delight because it demonstrates that the person likes you and wants to be generous and giving. It also highlights something positive about you, so that you can appreciate it, too. A seemingly little thing, like a compliment, can actually mean a great deal.

Instant happy

ENJOY!
Enjoy any compliments you're given and say, 'thank you' warmly.

Drifting off into a good night's sleep is a lovely feeling, as is waking up refreshed and ready to get up and go. Sleep requirements vary from one person to another, but most of us need around seven hours per night.

Sleep as well as you can because getting enough good-quality sleep is crucial to your health and wellbeing and fatigue may sabotage your happiness. Have you noticed that you feel a lot happier when you're fully rested and full of energy?

If you feel you need help to establish a sleep-well habit read a good self-help book on the subject or find out if there is a sleep clinic in your neighborhood.

Repeat performance

Watch a favorite film; one that you enjoy no matter how many times you've already see it. Each time the dialogue will be more familiar and more pleasing. Your relationship with the characters will deepen, and because you know what's going to happen, you can relax and luxuriate in the story and scenery. Sheer unadulterated pleasure.

Think 'bonhomie'

Think of the French word 'bonhomie' to put a smile in your mind and love in your heart. It means good will and a happy, warm attitude toward others. It makes for compassion and understanding, does away with social squalls like road or supermarket rage, and feels simply wonderful.

If there's something creative you want to do but keep deferring, you're probably a bit scared of it. This could apply to creative writing, painting a picture or making a present for someone. The secret is just to jump right in.

If you are writing something, just putting a few words, any words, down will get you going. Otherwise place some abstract brushstrokes on a canvas, or play a run of random notes on a musical instrument. You've all your future to change, practice and hone. For now, right this moment, all you have to do is begin. Enjoy the good feeling it gives you! Happiness is beginning. It's the essential element of anything that you try to achieve.

Wherever you have different people together you have different personalities interacting. You're sure, at least occasionally, to experience a clash of differing views from time to time. Sometimes this may escalate and become a clash of wills and suddenly your equilibrium is upset. You may feel as though you are on an emotional seesaw.

The secret to regaining your balance fast is to realize what is happening, accept that it's OK to differ, and think positively about resolving the situation. You could negotiate a solution or agree to live happily with the differences. Either way you'll feel better immediately.

Lulls between action are breathing spaces for quiet happiness to take place. In between having the dream and making the plans that lead to its realization, you'll have many times where nothing seems to be happening.

Take heart; lulls are all part of the process. They give you a valuable space in which to be happy as you reflect on your progress and ponder the steps you need to take to move forward. Or simply use the time to enjoy chilling out and refresh yourself by trying out something completely different.

It's often good to get out of your comfort zone. A challenging activity will let you see what you are really capable of and contribute to your self-confidence in every way. On top of this, doing something that deeply excites you gives you a brilliant high and is amazingly satisfying, too.

Think about what would stretch your comfort limits big time. Perhaps an extreme sport such as bungee-jumping or a challenging participation sport like ocean-racing might appeal to you? Whatever gives you a slight tingle of fear at the same time as the thought 'But boy, wouldn't it be amazing?' is a signal to go ahead and do it! Obviously you will need to get good training and take all the appropriate safety precautions, but do it. It will feel so, so good.

207

Have a pillow fight

Having a play pillow fight with your partner or friend is a great way to release anger and tension and get your relationship back on track again.

Soft, rounded pillows that won't hurt anyone are ideal for a mad game. Swatting each other with them will have you playing and giggling like a couple of kids; a breath of fresh air and fun in our oh-so-serious world.

Be your own best friend

The choice is yours. You have the power and the ability to be your own best friend or your own worst enemy. Forget the latter and cherish your inner best friend. She'll stick up for you, give you wise advice, comfort you and inspire you. She'll help you develop your confidence and self-esteem. She'll be there with you all through your life and, with her, you'll know great happiness.

Sometimes you'll find that you grasp a concept easily; perhaps something your partner or friend can't even begin to understand. You may try to explain it to them. But however well meant, any attempt to force them to catch up with you will worry them and probably make them dig their heels in more firmly. They'll engage with your ideas if and when they're ready to, and not before. Meanwhile, enjoy being with, and expanding, your own understanding.

Focal points are important in your home. They can be small and temporary, such as a vase of flowers on a table top, or large and permanent, such as an open fireplace with a collection of ornaments on the mantelpiece. Such focal points are places to gather around and they attract and hold the attention. Visually appealing, they give you a great feeling of being centered when you are relaxing at home. If you meditate, they can become focuses for your open-eyed gaze.

If you have a proper functioning fireplace, light a fire whenever you can. It's warming emotionally as well as physically and it's engrossing to watch real flames flickering brightly. If not, group your seating around some other attractive focal point such as a statue of the Buddha or an arrangement of driftwood and natural found objects.

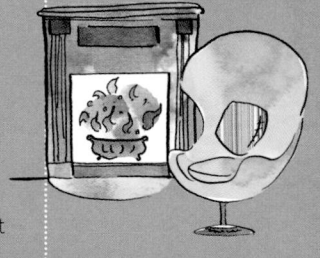

Look after long-term friendships that have stood the test of time with tender loving care, for they are part of your history and part of your happiness.

Treasure the shared history of your longstanding friendships for the mix of mutual memories, ongoing support and loyalty; it all weaves a wonderful fabric of love. You know each other very well, perhaps in many ways better than anyone else and that feels very, very good.

Surround yourself with the aura of a scent, not because it's fashionable or expensive, but because you just love it and it's special for you.

Whether the scent you choose is one you always wear, or one of many that appeal to you, it will harmonize with the natural perfume of your skin, becoming a fragrance unique to you. It will lift your spirits through the day and the pleasure will gently waft to others as well. Just lovely.

Instant happy

A-SCENT
A fragrance that you love is a direct a-scent to happiness.

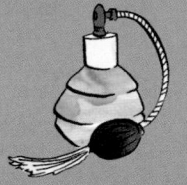

Keep people in the loop

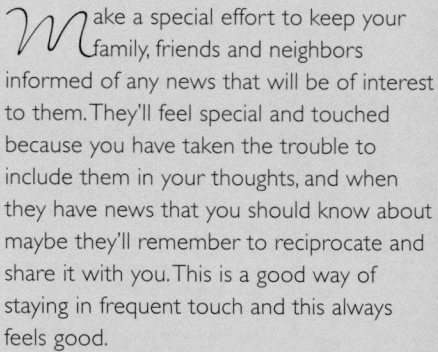

Make a special effort to keep your family, friends and neighbors informed of any news that will be of interest to them. They'll feel special and touched because you have taken the trouble to include them in your thoughts, and when they have news that you should know about maybe they'll remember to reciprocate and share it with you. This is a good way of staying in frequent touch and this always feels good.

Keeping each other 'in the loop' feels good for everyone and creates a warm sense of community.

Feel your spirits soaring when you sing, but have you ever tried singing in harmony with others? It takes the singing experience to new levels. Try harmonizing with your partner, relatives or friends or perhaps you could join a choir.

There is something magical about the way the notes work together to produce a gorgeous blend of sound. As well as being extremely satisfying to be part of such exciting music-making and having the fun of working together as a team, the harmonies resonate with the pleasure frequencies in your body. Just wondrous.

Instant happy

MANNERS TODAY
When you are traveling to work or going shopping, make a special point of holding doors open for people, regardless of whether they 'need' it or not.

Are good manners old-fashioned? No; they're an essential part of living happily with others and they help the world to run more smoothly. Manners aren't about alien or outdated etiquette, they are simply about putting others and yourself at ease and acting with consideration.

Whether you're lucky enough to learn manners through being coached by your parents and teachers, by reading books or magazines or from using your own common sense, courtesy feels truly comfortable and kindness always feels good.

If you've never tried volunteering for anything, why not give it a go? You can be a mentor, a hospital or hospice visitor, or perhaps you can help out in a thrift shop. There are many organizations that need your help. As well as assisting others, which is good for them, of course, volunteering is a direct route to your own personal happiness, too.

You meet all sorts of people whose paths otherwise might not have crossed yours, providing a wealth of interest for both parties. Your feelings and skills will be stretched, which feels good, too. And the satisfaction you derive will be immense.

Instant happy

TWO-WAY BENEFIT
Helping others brings happiness to you as well as to them.

Watch water

Walk by a stream or river and enjoy looking into the water, watching the way it flows, ripples and eddies. The beauty, sense of timelessness and the wildlife that abounds are all delights. The sound of the water is soothing, too. If you can swim or dangle your feet in, so much the better.

Your effort counts

Whatever you do, whether or not it's something you're good at, do your best. Positivity and willingness to try, along with effort put in, is what counts. It's life-enriching, feels good and, who knows, you may find you've greater potential or an ability you didn't even know you had.

List the good things

Make a special time every day, especially if you're feeling sorry for yourself, to draw up a list of all the good things in your life. This could include anything at all: a kindness shown to you or by you, a new purchase or a nice meal you've cooked. It could be the love that you enjoy in your life: your love for others or theirs for you. Once you start to make your list, a myriad of things will pop into your mind. Warm to your blessings, give thanks, be glad.

Instant happy

COUNT YOUR BLESSINGS
Recognizing how blessed you are makes your good fortune sing.

Count your blessings, count them one by one, and it will surprise you what the Lord has done.

Johnson Oatman Jr

Whenever you feel inexplicably troubled, reason your way around it. Reasoning calms you down and usually rapidly identifies the cause of your unhappiness.

Once you've got to the root of the matter, think of ways in which to remedy the problem and hopefully resolve it for good. Facing up to what's really wrong and looking into it allows you to stay upbeat and positive.

Food for the birds

A simple everyday act such as putting some crumbs out for the birds will raise your happiness levels. When you do this you know that you're doing your bit to help them thrive in hard times.

It's fascinating to watch birds and notice the way they communicate. You'll soon recognize certain individuals coming back for more every day. Their darting movements around the bird table or hanging feeder make an enticing picture show, too.

Instant happy

WINGED HAPPINESS
When you invite garden birds to feed, happiness flies into your life, too.

How did you do?

Whether you tried out several ideas this month or just one, you might like to reflect on what you chose to try and why, and if it worked for you.

1. How many activities did you try this month?

- 1–3 activities ☐
- 4–10 activities ☐
- 11–20 activities ☐
- 21–30 activities ☐

2. How many did you repeat several times in the month?

- 1–3 activities ☐
- 4–10 activities ☐
- 11–20 activities ☐
- 21–30 activities ☐

3. Which activities had a positive effect on your mood this month?

Use the page opposite to make notes about what worked for you and what didn't.

Notes, jottings and thoughts

A RECIPE FOR HAPPINESS
Conversation, laughter and good food shared is a great recipe for happiness.

Have a few friends round for supper. This simple act isn't so much about what you eat, though of course wholesome food, however simple, is a pleasure in its own right. Happiness also comes from knowing you've given your friends pleasure by inviting them, from your own gladness that they've made the effort to come, and, of course, from the pleasure of their company, too.

Make a list of all the things you'd like to do before you die.

Don't think of this as a negative activity, but one that will empower you to take a serious look at your life, where it's going and what it's for.

It's fine to include some impossible things. You'll have great fun thinking about them anyway. Then choose one that is actually viable and make plans to action it.

So often we look back on our lives and think 'If only I'd done that then.' From now on, be forward-thinking and constructive and ask yourself, 'What can I get going on now that, in the future, I'll be so pleased to have done?'

Instant happy

MAKE PLANS!
Something you want to do? Don't wait until it's too late. Do it now!

Hold the thought in your heart, even in your darkest times, that dawn always comes. Light always follows dark; hope always comes out of despair; even the bleakest of circumstances can improve.

When you see things in this new light, previously unfathomable situations and issues become clearer, enabling you to see ways to move forward. Keep this knowledge in your heart and it will give you gladness in bleak times.

Night's icy fingers flee as jocund day stands tiptoe on the misty mountain tops.

William Shakespeare

Instant happy

LOOK FOR LIGHT
When you feel as though you're in the dark and can't see much, take heart and look for the light. It will come.

ook at the world through rose-colored glasses. They'll help you see the bright side of things, the best of people, the humor in a situation. They'll fill you with enthusiasm and the feeling that you'll cope, no matter what.

Like anyone else, you'll have your share of sorrows and disappointments in your life. No one escapes this. But you'll weather them better and your life as a whole will be all the happier for your optimistic outlook.

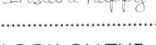

Instant happy

LOOK ON THE BRIGHT SIDE
A rosy outlook lets you see everything in the best light and it feels good too.

Do you and your partner or friend know what each other's favorite things are? Why not have fun with a personal quiz that is unique to your relationship? The answers will give you loads to talk about and it will feel great to fill each other in on all the things you're not aware of. This will help to deepen your knowledge of each other. Have an update every now and then as it's also fascinating to see how you're both changing.

Be a pilgrim

Think of yourself as a pilgrim on life's journey. Along the way, enjoy the company of others and learn from your experiences and theirs.

Seeing each day as a journey, you'll understand the promise at the start and look out for good things happening right the way through. With a pilgrim's sense of being on a quest for spiritual development, sense, too, the wonder of life.

Use the gift of sight — don't miss a thing and share the joy with others.

David Baird

Have a go at painting purely for fun, even if you haven't picked up a brush or a crayon since your school days. This exercise isn't about being 'good' at art, it's about playing.

You might like to try soft pastels, as they are brilliant for instant results, especially if you're inexperienced, but any medium is fine to try. Use whatever colors sing out to you and put them on the paper however you wish. It's up to you whether you do something abstract, impressionistic or realistic. Just enjoy the colors, shapes and the feel of the paint, pastels or crayons.

It's important to accept that we all have different standards of living, different talents and different luck in life. Once you know this, you'll find that you are able to cut out feelings of envy and jealousy and those 'poor me' thoughts, and this can be a huge relief. Once you are released from comparing yourself with others, you're free to enjoy everything you have and to use all your abilities and possibilities as opportunities for your ongoing happiness.

Today's thought

GIVE UP!
Giving up making comparisons frees you up to be happy just to be you.

A small success every day gives you a lift that lasts right through to the next one. This could take any form. Perhaps you have unexpectedly found something you wanted at the shops, so satisfying your hunter–gatherer instinct. Or perhaps you have managed to write a letter that you've been meaning to pen for ages. Or maybe you've tried out a recipe that sounded delicious, and it was.

You'll come up with heaps of ideas of your own. Just thinking, 'OK, what am I going to succeed at today?' feels great.

Be nice to people

If you live with other people, make a point of being nice to them. Cultivate a pleasant, feel-good closeness. Living together in an atmosphere of mutual respect, praise, encouragement, support and, of course, love, is a very real kind of heaven on Earth.

What would you miss?

Loved ones are a huge part of your happiness. Imagine that one of them was no longer around. What would you miss? Their presence, shared love, fun, conversations? Their voice? Their face? Their faults? Appreciate every moment you have. Love them and appreciate their love.

Give your day structure

Whether you're at work, studying or unemployed, having a structure to your day is very important and adds to your happiness and satisfaction.

So every morning make a rough or detailed plan of how the day will pan out. Be ambitious about how much you can get done within a certain period, by all means, but not so ambitious that you give up before you begin. Make your plan do-able.

Be sure to include some tasks you love and other treats to help the day go with a happy rhythm and swing.

Take the wilder route

Sometimes, when you have two choices, one will be safe and perhaps conventional, while the other will need courage and maybe a degree of wildness thrown in for good measure.

Happiness for much of your life will probably mean following an expected path, especially if you have responsibility for children. But hey, it's fantastic, at least now and then in life, to take the wilder way.

Two roads diverged in a wood, and I — I took the one less traveled by, and that has made all the difference.

Robert Frost

Today's thought

LISTEN TO GUT FEELINGS

When you get a gut feeling to take a different route, trust it. It will give you great satisfaction.

Do something different; take a boat trip. Whether it's in a motor boat or a sailing boat, you'll experience the freedom of the open water and the wind in your hair. Whether it's at sea or on a lake, there's nothing like the feeling of the wind taking the sails or a powerful motor zipping the boat along.

The wind in your face, the salt spray and the freedom are all exhilarating. And the sense of harnessing the energy of the elements in a sailing boat will do wonders for your self-confidence. You'll feel at peace with nature. Above all it's sheer, wonderful fun.

When storm clouds gather, either in reality or metaphorically, you take sensible steps to prepare for them. If it rains, for example, you put on a waterproof and boots. If it's cold you wrap up warm. If it freezes, you turn up the heating.

The same applies to inclement emotional climes; you'll find there's always a remedy. You can take shelter and lie low for a while or you can be brave and get to grips with whatever's being thrown at you. If you use all your resources you'll find it's easier to get through life's difficult patches and you'll feel happier into the bargain.

Today's thought

THE SUN WILL COME OUT AGAIN

Whenever storms threaten or rage around you, cope as best you can, but always remember that the Sun will come out again. This feels highly empowering.

day 228

Don't dish the dirt

DON'T BE AFRAID TO BE NICE

When someone's being ridiculed, refuse to join in and when possible stand up for them. Ignore cynics who tease you for being too nice. Being nice feels good.

Make a big effort not to dish the dirt about other people, even if others denounce you as a 'Pollyanna'. It always unsettles people when they realize they're being unpleasant and gossipy.

Check whether you're honestly not being self-righteous or priggish and stop doing it if you are. Then say to yourself (and them if they keep teasing you), 'Hey, Pollyanna was great! She was happy and much loved; what's not to like?'

ave you ever made use of that wonderful phenomenon 'the second wind'? This is where you feel you've spent all your energy and can no long go on, but then you find you have some spare energy reserves to draw on.

When you're exercising you'll recognize a moment when it ceases to feel difficult and instead feels pleasurable, almost effortless. It's a fantastic feeling. Get used to going for that second-wind feeling in anything demanding you're doing. It could be any project at work or home. Push through initial resistance and love the way you suddenly get into gear and start enjoying yourself. Great!

When you read a novel you love, imagine you're going to direct the film version of it. Have fun thinking about how you'd plan the scenes and sets. Which actors would you choose for the main roles? Now visualize the opening night. Who would you invite to watch the premiere with you? What would you wear and what sort of party would you have afterwards? Enjoy the creative, thrilling dream. Deciding how you'd film a book you love and who you'd have in it is a dreamy way of extending the pleasure.

When your smile for someone is genuine, accompanying, that is, a kind thought or warm greeting, the pleasure of their response will reflect back on to you. You'll notice that it feels physically and emotionally good to smile; lifting the muscles of your face relaxes not just your face, but your whole stance and it triggers feel-good chemicals in your brain, too.

Today's thought

TODAY, JUST SMILE
Smile at people. Every time you do you'll feel pleasure and send some to them, too.

Somebody smiled at me today
Somebody's face was kind,
It's surprising how good a smile
can be
It leaves all the dark clouds
behind.

Paula Roberts

241

Buy lots of fresh fruit and pile it up in a beautiful big fruit bowl on the kitchen table. Every time you look at it you'll feel a surge of happiness because it looks so wholesome and tempting; like a fantastic edible painting.

Fruit symbolizes providence and plenty, so that's a lovely thought, too. And of course it tastes wonderful and is very good for you. It's good all round in the happiness stakes.

There's huge satisfaction in learning a technical skill, especially one that you thought was totally implausible for you. You could take up a traditional craft like carpentry, or something contemporary like internet technology. For maximum pleasure score, choose something that feels alien to you and which you're a bit scared of doing. Your sense of achievement as you're learning and finally mastering a new skill is great. And yes, you can do it. Take it gently, step by step, and you'll get there just fine!

Always let go of a grievance last thing at night. Don't go to sleep on an argument. Make it up with your partner or dismiss any annoyance between you before you drop off to sleep.

If you've fallen out with a friend or colleague, write on a piece of paper a pledge to sort it all out in the morning, and say a prayer for peace and resolution. That way your subconscious will get to work on ways to find peace and/or a resolution of differences while you happily drift off into sweet dreams.

Enjoy saying both 'Yes' and 'No' to food. Savoring just one small piece of carrot cake rather than gorging on two big bits is highly pleasurable and proves your ability to enjoy, but sensibly limit, your indulgence; satisfying all round. Being aware of how much is good for you doesn't detract one iota from your pleasure; accepted, it heightens not only the deliciousness but does wonders for your self-esteem, too.

Today's thought

REMOVING GUILT
When you know you can say 'No' as well as 'Yes' you'll find that the guilt factor disappears, leaving your pleasure at the deliciousness intact.

When depression happens, as it can to anyone, mix your own recipe for distractions and healing strategies to speed its departure and restore happiness. Speed up depression's departure by thinking what you can do to give yourself some respite from it.

First, it's good to consult your doctor; then you could, for instance, dance, sleep, do some voluntary work or talk with a counsellor. Meditation's extraordinarily healing, too, and so is reading books by others who've been where you are now but have come through.

Last, but not least, as your depression lifts, welcome happiness back in with open arms.

reat yourself as you would like others to treat you; that is, kindly, encouragingly, caringly and lovingly.

By being considerate to yourself as well as others, you'll set a positive example for them to follow. Seeing your self-respect in action, they'll be far more likely to treat you well. And by being good to yourself you'll naturally create a great environment for happiness. Enjoy it.

Today's thought

LET IT FLOW
Happiness flows when you treat yourself lovingly.

Kick out anger

When something is over that meant a lot to you: a relationship, a happy time or a job, don't cling to it, move on to the next stage of life. Appreciate the good fortune you've had, but defuse lingering possessiveness and kick out any anger. Doesn't that feel better? Yes, you can be happy again!

day 239

Give a warm welcome

When someone visits, give them a warm welcome and turn the TV or radio off. They'll feel honored, and you won't have to compete for attention. Receive their company as a gift. Focus on each other with interest and warmth. The visit will be a time of great happiness.

Enjoy your life, good fortune, talents and abilities to the full. Relish your achievements and show your happiness. Being glad for your light gives others the chance to share your enthusiasm and joy. Be open about your abilities and your delight in life. Welcoming your happiness with a glad flourish will encourage it to stay or at least visit you often. Your openness will help others more than you think.

> *We are all meant to shine, as children do. We were born to make manifest the glory of God that is within us.*
>
> Nelson Mandela

There is a time for work and a time for leisure, although sometimes work spills over into our leisure time. Make it a general rule that you have a clear boundary between them. That way, when you step over it into your leisure time, however you choose to relax, you will feel wholly free to enjoy yourself, and deservedly so. Your time of relaxation is to be guarded well and cherished. So when it's time to relax, enjoy it wholeheartedly.

*M*ostly, be patient. Once you relax into patience, it feels really good. Others, following your example, will relax too and so you create an atmosphere of calm and peaceful contentment as you wait. In time, people and things progress at the pace that's right for them, so why worry? Sometimes, a situation cries out to be changed right now, in which case impatience can get things rolling. But, usually, a gently, gently approach works best, and makes for happiness all round.

Today's thought

BENEFITS
Patience is a benefit in most situations, especially to your equilibrium.

Whether you tried out several ideas this month or just one, you might like to reflect on what you chose to try and why, and if it worked for you.

1. How many activities did you try this month?

- 1–3 activities ☐
- 4–10 activities ☐
- 11–20 activities ☐
- 21–30 activities ☐

2. How many did you repeat several times in the month?

- 1–3 activities ☐
- 4–10 activities ☐
- 11–20 activities ☐
- 21–30 activities ☐

3. Which activities had a positive effect on your mood this month?

Use the page opposite to make notes about what worked for you and what didn't.

Notes, jottings and thoughts

Playing cards is interesting, sociable, mind-stretching and great fun, so invite your family or some friends to join you in a few games. It's a great opportunity to take part in something as a group, and people who play cards together often form great bonds with each other.

As well as being a pleasure in the moment, the experience is so vivid and the laughter and competition so vibrant that you'll remember particular games years later, evoking the happiness that you felt that day.

When you have a shock or accident, it's easy to feel 'Why me?' Instead of this automatic response, ask yourself 'Why not me?' and you instantly stop feeling like a victim.

We live in a world where happenstance is often random, but we are far from being helpless. Whatever befalls you, you have the ability to deal with it the best way you can. Strength will come to help you through and eventually happiness will come back again.

Writing spontaneously every day gets your creative juices flowing, setting you up to have a successful day, whatever you are doing. Get into the routine of writing two or three pages daily. It's best to do this by hand, maybe in your regular journal, but write on-screen if it's easier for you.

Simply spill out whatever comes into your mind. Let the words flow and you'll soon find that they will. Sometimes what you write might be gobbledegook, but at other times you may get into telling a story, recording journal notes or perhaps even writing some stunning prose or poetry. This will give you a buzz of happiness at the time, and for years to come you can mine your store of writing for the best bits. It's a truly uplifting activity.

For feel-good, meaningful conversations, make an effort to talk the same language. Otherwise you may end up talking at cross-purposes, which is confusing for both parties. It's all too tempting to charge ahead, repeating yourselves and getting annoyed with each other. Instead, slow down and think, 'OK, how can we explain ourselves and understand each other better?'

Often the simple answer is for you both to listen carefully to each other instead of fretting about what you're going to say next. And when it is your turn to speak, say what you're trying to explain another way. Suddenly, you'll be in tune. You'll be speaking and listening on the same wavelength: it feels fantastic.

Positive, happy talk surely is the beginning of many a dream coming true. Talking through your aspirations with your partner or someone else you trust, gives your ideas and optimism free rein to express themselves. You'll be given the space to help you think plans through carefully, too. This keeps your spirit of adventure and anticipation alive.

Happy happy, happy talk.
Talk about things you'd like to
do... If you don't have a
dream, how you goin' to make
your dreams come true?

Rogers and Hammerstein

It's fun to get hands-on at something practical and doing something useful and giving your home a present feels good, too. The feeling of success when you've finished will tick all your happiess boxes. So if you have some things that need doing around your home, have a go at a little do-it-yourself.

When you get stuck into a project, everything from the initial idea, through the visit to the store for materials, to actually carrying the job out gives you a great sense of purpose. The momentum of happiness carries right on after you've finished, with an ongoing sense of achievement!

Today's thought

CELEBRATE WITH FOOD

Eating slowly turns even the simplest meal into a celebration.

Our food is one of the great pleasures in life, so make the most of it by eating slowly; the experience will add to your happiness. To do this you need to chew thoroughly; chewing well not only gives you the chance to enjoy the taste as fully as possible, but helps your digestion. The end result will be a sense of unhurried calm and enjoyment.

When you have something to eat, be sure to sit down at a proper table, rather than eating on the hoof. Lay the table properly. In between mouthfuls, put your cutlery down to remind you that there's no hurry.

Accept others, especially your loved ones, just as they are. You'll find that your lack of judgment will make you feel a lot more contented. Even if you could force, or coerce, a person into changing their ways as you wish, there's a good chance that they'd revert to their own path in time. They might resent being controlled by you, too.

The best way of influencing someone is to set a good example. This might encourage the person to emulate you. Give them your opinion and advice if they ask you for it. Otherwise relax; let them be and love them as they are.

Instant happy

LEAVE ALONE
Let your own happiness glow by letting others be themselves.

ind happiness in your past, your present and in your future. Enjoy the ever-present afterglow of the good things from your past, happy memories, for example, and experiences of love and fulfilment.

Anticipate the future with a joyful heart and walk into it with hope and faith that all will be well. Today enjoy or learn from everything that happens. Feel yourself in the flow as much as possible and give thanks for the day.

A happy anthology

Make an anthology of things that make you happy. Start off with whatever you already love and add anything you come across or that happens in your life that gives you a thrill or glow of pleasure. It could be any kind of happiness, from quiet agreement, through contentment, to wondrous euphoria.

Be curious

Have boundless curiosity about life: our world, what makes us tick, what makes others tick. Irrepressible fascination with our extraordinary world is an eternal source of enjoyment. Learn all the time. This feels great and the more your knowledge and wisdom grow, the better it gets.

Feel fit

Feeling fit and loving the size you are; big, small or somewhere in between, is a great way to add to your personal happiness. Whatever your shape and general health, enjoy keeping yourself as fit as is reasonably possible. 'Reasonably' is important, by the way, as all-round health is all about enjoying keeping fit.

Beware of going over the top on either exercising or dieting. Happy health is all about looking after yourself well, in particular keeping your muscles toned, your body in all-round good shape and eating food that does you good and tastes wonderful, too.

If you feel comfortable, you're more likely to feel happier in yourself. So dress for comfort as much as for style; the two can even go together!

When you wear clothes that hang well and aren't too tight or too baggy, you feel free, poised and relaxed. Comfort does wonders for your confidence and you'll also find that you can really enjoy whatever you're wearing, feel pleased with the way you look and be glad that you chose well. You'll feel as though you can conquer the world.

Having an ambitious goal that requires much training and discipline pays back a thousand-fold in terms of the flow of harnessed energy and determination. Its effects can make your spirit sing.

The sense of achievement is immense through all the months of training, both on the finishing line and long afterwards. Your fortitude as you keep going, despite the physical challenges and pressures, gives a tremendous sense of your strength of character. And yes, the joy is euphoric.

Run a marathon — it gives you an amazing sense of achievement and such a sense of joy it's hard to describe.

Richard Lawrence

Let people know you like them, and notice that they like you, too. It will make everyone happy, all round. Once in a class, the teacher pinned a piece of paper to everyone's back. All the individuals then went round writing on each one why they liked that person. It was good to focus on the things they liked and each person was totally amazed to read the wonderful things written about them. It was heaven.

Realize, now, that you're much loved and admired and let others know how much you value them, too.

Today's thought

YOU ARE MUCH LOVED
Be aware of how much others like you, in so many different ways.

Love as fully as you can

TAKE THE PLUNGE
Be brave and dare to love wholeheartedly; love is worth it and so are you.

*L*ove as though you've never been, or will be, hurt. It feels so different that you may be amazed to realize how guarded you've been up until this point. It's a natural reaction to think, 'If I don't let myself love I can't be hurt.' In actual fact, preventing yourself from loving as fully as possible only hurts yourself.

We all need to love. It's quite true that there are no guarantees when it comes to love and you might get hurt, but you'll heal, too. So take the risk of loving; it's a part of being alive and part of your personal happiness.

Build bridges

Be prepared to build bridges in your life. They are a joy to cross, and it's great when others come to join us from the other side.

Even if you've fallen out with someone and they don't want to make it up now, or they're avoiding you for some reason you're unaware of, be ready to welcome them back into your life if they'd like to be friends again.

It feels good to know you're not holding a grudge, and if you do make it up, that will feel good, too.

Today's thought

BUILD PEACE
A willingness to make up and be friends builds a bridge across a rift between friends and gives you a comforting sense of peace.

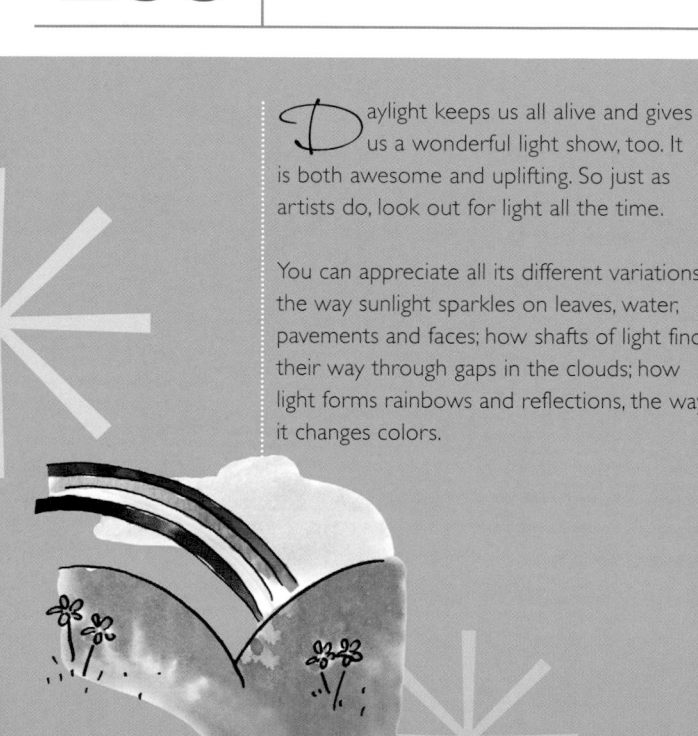

aylight keeps us all alive and gives us a wonderful light show, too. It is both awesome and uplifting. So just as artists do, look out for light all the time.

You can appreciate all its different variations: the way sunlight sparkles on leaves, water, pavements and faces; how shafts of light find their way through gaps in the clouds; how light forms rainbows and reflections, the way it changes colors.

*L*ast thing in the evening, a late hot drink makes you feel warm, snug and sleepy. If you like milk, it's a good choice as it's a natural tranquilizer and so is chamomile tea.

Sipped slowly, alone or curled up on the sofa with a partner, it feels like you're being kind to yourself. It's also a soothing routine that helps you wind down and prepare for the night ahead.

It was once the custom to tithe a percentage of your income to the poor and today it still feels every bit as good to give to charity. As well as the obvious benefits to others, you'll feel good, too. So tithe some of your income or time to charity and feel the happiness of doing your bit for others.

However, it's important not to overstretch and give beyond your means. Remember that if you don't currently have the wherewithal to give money, fundraising or other voluntary work is just as generous and lifts your spirits high, too.

Sink into some healing music. Many of the great composers, classical and modern, believed that their music came or comes to them from another dimension. This explains the power music has over people and its emotional appeal.

Scientists have discovered that particular melodies, cadences and rhythms resonate with the healing ability of our brains and bodies. Mozart, Brahms, Bob Dylan and Enya spring to mind, but you must choose the composer or musician who strikes a healing chord with you.

Instant happy

LISTEN TO MUSIC
The more we listen to music with healing power, the more we realize that it makes us feel better. It can feel like floating in happiness.

Transcendence, the understanding that there is more to the universe than we are aware of, acknowledges other dimensions, which even sceptical scientists agree are yet to be discovered.

Whatever your views, try to delight in the mystery of the universe and reach out toward it, for underlying the theory is a respect for all other sentient creatures and for our planet. A sense of reverence and resonance with the mindfulness behind it all gives great happiness and serenity.

Theology, biology and philosophy pursued in harmony are the foundation of natural religion.

Anon

There is something enchanting about feet, or rather the shoes, socks and tights we wear on them. There's no need to go crazy about them like Imelda, but do take care to choose shoes that give your heart a little (or big) leap of joy whenever you happen to look down at them. Those who don't understand the fascination might scoff, but to those of us in the know, shoes are sooooo good!

Instant happy

SHOE HAPPINESS
Why wear boring shoes, socks and tights when you can choose footwear that absolutely delights you?

Today's thought

AMICABLE
With the word 'amicable' at the front of your mind and heart, pain can't turn to bitterness and healing can restore your happiness soon.

If a relationship turns sour, don't get stuck in a cycle of blame and anger. Step clear of the strife, refusing to row any more or obsess about it. The neutral space this provides will give you a chance to remember the love you shared, and perhaps still do share. Inspiration will then flow in to heal the hurt and resolve or manage differences amicably.

Ever has it been that love knows not its own depth until the hour of separation.

Kahlil Gibran

When someone does something for you, put everything you've got into an enthusiastic response. In saying something like, 'You're a star; thank you so much!' You'll give the person great pleasure and they'll feel your appreciation to the full. You'll also encourage them and others, including yourself, to continue doing your best for each other.

*L*obby for democracy at home and at work. Democracy, where everyone is valued and can have their say in how things are run, is a comfortable and nurturing place to be. Everyone has a chance to blossom and the natural leaders, or those who must lead, such as the boss or the parents, come naturally to the fore, well supported by the others.

It's true! You really can make a difference! You can reduce your carbon footprint in all kinds of ways. You can do some voluntary work for a charity that helps in war-torn countries. You can tell your politician your views on how to encourage global peace, interaction and solidarity. You can be a force for positivity in your neighborhood. You can help look after the countryside and our wildlife. Quietly or loudly, you can help the world. Know this and your heart will sing with hope for a better future.

| Being in love

*B*eing in love is mostly about hormones and pheromones, but it often feels magically as though you're in heaven. It's wondrous.

Then there is love based on true compatibility, deep liking and ongoing physical attraction. It isn't as giddy or euphoric and won't always feel like heaven, but actually it's about the nearest we get to Heaven on this Earth. Enjoy every second.

The Wow! factor

Have some of the Wow! factor today. Look out for things that really surprise or move you. If you look for them, you'll find them in just about everything that you are doing. You might read something that makes you go 'Wow, that's interesting!' or 'Wow, what amazing writing!' for instance. Or you might have some unexpected good luck, or bump serendipitously into a friend; it could be anything. The trick is to notice it and think 'Wow!' and you'll magnify the happiness you experience.

We'll just have to keep on singing.

Rolf Harris

Life isn't always an oasis of peace. In fact, it can be pretty awful at times. But when you soldier bravely on through even the worst of times with a fighting spirit, survivor mentality and hope in your heart, singing as you go, the singing somehow transcends everything else. You'll find a joy unlike any other, probably because it's in such contrast to the negativity.

Put the world to rights with your friends or colleagues. Get a discussion going about anything that interests you or might if you started thinking about it. If it gets lively, enjoy the pace and thrust of the debate. Remember it's not personal; you're finding your way around all your different opinions and that's fascinating and great fun.

Today's thought

DISCUSS, DISCUSS AND DISCUSS AGAIN!

Discuss all kinds of topics. It makes you think, increases your understanding of the subject and those you're talking with, and makes you all feel involved and engaged.

How did you do?

*W*hether you tried out several ideas this month or just one, you might like to reflect on what you chose to try and why, and if it worked for you.

1. How many activities did you try this month?

- 1–3 activities
- 4–10 activities
- 11–20 activities
- 21–31 activities

2. How many did you repeat several times in the month?

- 1–3 activities
- 4–10 activities
- 11–20 activities
- 21–31 activities

3. Which activities had a positive effect on your mood this month?

Use the page opposite to make notes about what worked for you and what didn't.

Notes, jottings and thoughts

Instant happy

HAVE A SYMBOL
A symbol of contentment in your home, such as a beautiful vase of flowers, will encourage you to create good vibrations with a positive, loving attitude.

A simple thing, but one we often neglect, is to be glad that we're alive, from the moment we wake up to the time we go off to sleep at night.

Waking up means you get to enjoy this amazing world and its wealth of experiences one more time. Every morning, rejoice with all your heart at a new day to explore and put your all into enjoying yourself.

Have a regular survey

Instead of cruising through life on auto-pilot, have a regular survey or 'life audit'. Check out where you are, where you're going and how everything feels. It's a good idea to monitor what's going well and what's not. And it gives you the chance to plan any changes of direction that come up on the radar as a good idea.

Instant happy

IN CONTROL
A regular survey of your life puts you at the controls of forward-planning and that feels fantastic.

Nobody can go back and start a new beginning, but anyone can start today and make a new ending.
Maria Robinson

287

Place a cluster of citrine stones in the southwest corner of your home. They symbolize happiness and harmony in the household and they draw away negative emotions, creating feelings of safety. They also energize and invigorate, restoring energy resources wherever they are needed.

If the idea of crystals doesn't appeal to you you could choose an object that's special to you, representing a good time in your life or something beloved by you. It will give you pleasure every time you're close by. This could be an ornament, a piece of sculpture or something you've brought back from a special holiday.

Even if you've never tried before and think you lack poetic ability, try writing a poem. Now! Just drop a few words on to the page or play around with them in your mind and feel the pleasure.

You might like to experiment with a conventional structure of your choice, such as rhyming or rap. Or you could be wild and free and just aim for something that sounds good. You could express something deep or have fun with limericks. It's up to you. It's your unique poem and it spells happiness.

Instant happy

DAILY RHYME
A poem a day blows the blues away. (You'll do so much better!)

Instant happy

WONDER
Indulge yourself by learning about the natural wonders of the world and reveling in their beauty.

Contemplating the dazzling beauty of the natural wonders of the world stirs a feeling of awe for the sheer miracle of Creation.

You'll discover a kind of simplicity at work in the complexity. Each aspect of Creation is a pure and unquestionable work of sublime, supreme artistry. Take the Northern Lights, for example. So breathtakingly amazing, you just want to soak in the sight of them. The sights of Creation can make you feel inner happiness now and forever.

Listen to soothing sounds

Listen to the songs of nature: birds singing, the crooning of the wind, the rippling of a stream, waves on the shore. In evoking the timelessness and beauty of nature they give you a sense of belonging in the world.

The sound itself has its own joy and, like man-made music, resonates with something in us. In calming and healing us, it brings with it a quiet contentment.

Instant happy

LISTEN TO NATURE
The sounds of nature carry you on a special wavelength to happiness.

Instant happy

NIGHT-TIME PRAYERS

Handing concerns over relieves you of them. Everything looks better in the morning.

Night time is for sleep, relaxation, healing, and above all replenishment. By asking the universe, or God, to take over any outstanding issues while you rest, you can sleep undisturbed. Then you wake refreshed and full to the brim again, with the energy and capability to cope with whatever the day holds in store. Confidence restored, you feel so good.

Who are your special heroes? They could be people you know well and admire or complete strangers, perhaps famous people, who inspire you. Whenever you yearn for a leader, but can't find one, think of the hero who would be perfect and imagine they are there with you. What would they say and do? Follow their lead and you will share their strength. It feels good to have heroes.

Instant happy

FOLLOW THE LEADER

Having a few heroes to look up to in your life is inspirational. Just thinking of them is strengthening and uplifting.

Which colors make your heart sing with happiness? Get to know your favorites, and which shade of them resonates most. Bring the colors you love to the forefront of your life. You could choose them in your clothes, soft furnishings and other interior decoration as well as in lots of small ways. Or you could buy some paints, set them out on a palette and have fun, like Matisse, creating your own colorist masterpiece.

Ask a prophet

If you're not sure what, morally, the right thing is, it quickly clarifies the situation if you imagine what one of the great religious leaders would advise. Asking yourself, for example, what Christ or Mohammed would say cuts out any judgmental attitudes which may have been prejudicing the question for you.

Be moderate

Moderation in all things is a good maxim for happiness. Too much of something good dulls the pleasure of it. Too little feels inadequate. Enough to please and satisfy is just perfect and the knowledge you know and keep to your self-set limits feels good in itself, too.

So often, in waiting for big, wonderful things to happen, you may fail to notice small occurrences. But noticing the small, mundane everyday happenings will make them light up your life.

For example, think about the small kind deeds done by you and others, every smile you give or receive and the laughter you enjoy. Every enthusiasm and inspiration shines, as does a beautiful thought or something touching you've observed.

Polish something

There's great satisfaction to be had from giving something a good polish. This could be silver, copper or brass, if you have some, or leather shoes, or a tiled floor or wooden furniture.

You'll be pleased with the end result, of course. Your tarnished or dulled item will look as good as new. But there's something very meditative about the actual motion of polishing; it just feels nice, especially as the shine begins to develop. And the satisfaction of seeing this makes you glow with happiness, too.

Today's thought

CONFIDENCE

- Think confident
- Be confident
- Look confident
- Inspire confidence

Adopt an 'I'm a leader' mindset and it will instantly be mirrored in your body language. You'll quickly feel more confident and therefore happier. Your whole demeanor, posture and movement will change and you'll look confident and capable. You'll inspire others so much that they'll feel safe and happy following your lead. This will feel just great for you and for all those around you.

As we look ahead into the next century, leaders will be those who empower others.

Bill Gates

Watch birds

The next time you have an opportunity, take time out to watch birds flocking together. Their precision flight is a miracle of communication, coordination and expertise. It's a ballet more beautiful than we humans could ever perform, and if you're lucky enough to be in quiet surroundings you'll hear the music of their flight path, too. Wondrous!

Watching birds fly in formation is just amazing — it makes me feel joyous.
Mary Wood

When you do a job on your own, enjoy the opportunity to be mindful, concentrating on the task in hand and relishing your commitment and focus.

When you work with someone else or with a team, enjoy coordinating your efforts, the speed at which you progress through the job, the camaraderie you share. Either way, work will be a pleasure.

Coming together is a beginning.
Keeping together is progress.
Working together is success.

Henry Ford

While mostly it's good to enjoy the present and look forward positively, every now and then it's nice to wallow in nostalgia for happy times in the past. You could get out old family photo albums, or in your mind walk around a beloved childhood home. Or you might like to watch some of the very first films you were taken to see or revisit haunts of your exciting teenage years. Wasn't it good and isn't it good to remember?

Instant happy

HAPPY TIMES
When you remember good times from the past, the feelings, relived, are often as joyous as they were at the time.

Do you ever long for fame and celebrity? Do you feel that these would make you feel happier than you are now? Well, you're just as likely to be happy living a quiet, uncelebrated life as you are if you're famous; probably more so.

Either way, the secret is to enjoy the way you are and not pine for something you haven't got. Sure, some celebrities enjoy fame, but many don't and suffer in their lives. Billions of people, though, are very happy leading simple, unassuming lives and enjoying their privacy.

ignity is all about making reasoned choices in life. So it's important to treasure your right and your ability to do so. Be glad to be making your path in your life in your own way; do your best in life and walk tall.

Hold fast to your dignity and don't let anyone or anything take it from you. It's also about being as compassionate to others as you are to yourself. Helping people to maintain their dignity feels good for you and for them, too.

day 293 Leave your fingerprint

Today's thought

YOUR MARK

Make your every mark on the world as beautiful as you can.

Whenever you do something lovingly, creatively or skilfully, you will leave your personal, completely individual imprint that will never be erased because it's a fixture in eternity. Doesn't that thought inspire you? Hold it in your heart and make your fingerprint, wherever it rests in the world, something you're proud is yours.

Snow is a real treat. Whatever your age, enjoying a snowfall will make you feel like a kid again. You could simply walk on it, relishing that special soft but crunchy feeling under your feet. You could play; snowball fights and tobogganing are brilliant. You may like to ski. If you're a beginner you'll laugh and laugh and laugh, and if you're experienced there are few other things quite as exhilarating as swooshing down a snowy slope.

Instant happy

WHITE WINTER OPPORTUNITY
If you get a surprise fall of snow or an unexpected chance to enjoy a white winter, take it!

Today's thought

BOOKS IN YOUR LIFE

The books that are your soul-mates are some of the key pieces in the jigsaw of life's happiness.

When a book speaks directly to you, it feels as though you and it were meant to for each other; and as though it was written to you or for you.

The characters and the messages of the book are very real to you. The first time you read it, you either can't put it down or, if you're very self-disciplined, you read just a little bit at a time, enjoying every sentence, to make it last longer. And every time you re-read it, it's more familiar, like a much-loved friend.

Now and again in a lifetime you discover a soul-book, a work that engraves itself on your heart: one you read over and over, falling in love with it more deeply each time.

Roger Deakin

Speak as thoughtfully and as wisely as you possibly can, at all times. Be tactful. When you tread on others' feelings remember they're as fragile as glass. Be a peacemaker and encourage tolerance and healing. Civilization would fall apart without diplomacy: it starts with you at home and is a strong foundation for happiness.

Do something today that you've never done before. It will refresh you and pep up your enthusiasm for life in general. You could, for instance, go to a shop you've never been to before or visit a museum. Or it could be something social like talking to someone you've never spoken with before. Trying out some new experiences is always interesting and fun and may even lead to new enthusiasms and inspirations.

It's so very easy to become cynical if you read or listen to the news a great deal, because a lot of it seems negative and this may make you feel you can't trust anyone. However, it's important to keep positive things in mind and be ready to trust others. Bad news hits the headlines because it's unusual. Good news abounds, but it's precisely because it's the norm that it isn't deemed newsworthy. Most people are kind-hearted and willing to do good whenever they can. They are trustworthy. Keep your wits about you, of course, but trust others as much as possible.

Today's thought

MOST PEOPLE ARE GOOD

Cynicism is misinformed as the vast majority of people are well-meaning. Trust is usually rewarded with goodness and it feels good.

Keep tabs

CARE FOR YOUR MIND

Caring for the health of your mind is just as vital and feels as good as keeping physically fit.

I t's important to keep tabs on your emotional and mental health. Every now and then review how you're feeling and think about how content you are with your life.

If you feel out of kilter in some way, think about how you can restore the balance. Perhaps you need more rest and relaxation. Or do you need to sort out issues in a relationship, change something at work or re-kindle your inspiration and creativity?

It feels good to focus on what's wrong and consider how you can help put things right.

Seek to mediate

day 300

Wherever there's conflict, there's hope for, and the possibility of, resolution. While we need to stand up and defend morality, truth and liberty, at the same time if you seek to mediate, mend and work toward a future that's good for everyone, you will be at peace within.

Give up something

day 301

Why not give up something you know is bad for you? It feels great to do something positive to oust a damaging habit. Get help, if need be. This could be support from someone who understands what you're going through. This feels good and is extremely therapeutic.

Enjoy the many pleasures of food. There's the anticipation of thinking about how good a meal will taste as you're shopping for the ingredients. You can enjoy setting the table, too, and of course the cooking itself.

If you think you find cooking boring, look to one of the TV cooks. They're a great inspiration. Think lovingly, too, of the pleasure you're providing for yourself and anyone else you're feeding.

The weather, with all its seasonal patterns and daily uncertainty, is a perennial source of interest. Because there are so many variations and contrasts most kinds of weather are enjoyable. There's the delight of the sunshine after days of cloud, for example, and the relief when it rains after a drought. Most of all, on the happiness front, it's a subject that connects us all, and that feels so good.

I love watching the seasons and comparing them, year by year, and the weather fascinates me — I enjoy forecasting and I'm told I'm very good at it.

Walter Price

313

Whether you tried out several ideas this month or just one, you might like to reflect on what you chose to try and why, and if it worked for you.

1. How many activities did you try this month?

* 1–3 activities
* 4–10 activities
* 11–20 activities
* 21–30 activities

2. How many did you repeat several times in the month?

* 1–3 activities
* 4–10 activities
* 11–20 activities
* 21–30 activities

3. Which activities had a positive effect on your mood this month?

Use the page opposite to make notes about what worked for you and what didn't.

314

Notes, jottings and thoughts

It always feels good to give praise and encouragement when it's due. So take a moment to think of all the things you need to appreciate about modern life. For example, aren't we privileged to have such outstanding public services?

The utilities and the infrastructure of modern life is generally extremely good. When you think about the post, for example, it's great to know that you can post a letter in one part of the country and within a day or two it will reach its destination.

Speed is exhilarating. The buzz you get from going fast or watching others race is incredibly exciting and the high lasts long after the instant rush of the moment. The rush of adrenaline makes your spirits soar and it's just great fun.

So instead of constantly pacing yourself at medium speed as you walk or jog, now and then put on a spurt and go as fast as you can. If you love to cycle, the same applies. If you're unable to participate yourself, watch others racing and let rip with your enthusiasm. Yes!

Today's thought

EAT WELL TO FEEL WELL

The goodness of your food will have a big impact on your emotional wellbeing.

Stress uses up vitamins, so you need an even better diet than usual if you're anxious about something or under a lot of pressure. Look after your mind by taking care to eat a varied diet of wholesome foods. Chosen well, they will give you all the nutrients you need as well as boosting your spirits with their deliciousness. Your food is as important to mental health as to your body. Taking care to eat healthily helps to fuel your capacity to be happy and it's good for your self-esteem, too.

When someone else is grumpy or non-communicative, don't take their mood on board. Staying neutral and good-humored will, if it's appropriate, help you to help them. But bear in mind they may have a sorrow or worry in their life that you don't know about. If you're calm and happy it will be far easier to be understanding and compassionate.

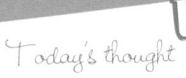

Today's thought

USE COMPASSION
Compassion means you won't resent other people's behavior and judge them harshly. As well as feeling a whole lot more comfortable for you, it will help them, too.

Just sing!

SING OUT
Throw your inhibitions to the winds and sing out like a songbird. It doesn't matter if you don't sound like one!

Have great fun and get into 'diva' mode by singing in the bath or singing along with a record. Bathrooms are well-known for their wonderful acoustics and they make your voice sound brilliant.

Karaoke also has the happy knack of convincing you that you were born to sing. Plenty of practice should have the benefit of improving your voice, but whatever the result, you will get maximum enjoyment.

When you're selling something, be prepared to negotiate, at least a little, on price. People love to feel they're getting a bargain and you'll feel generous and big-hearted, too.

And whenever you are doing well from a sale, give added value to the purchaser. You could, for instance, throw in a little extra as a free gift, or make an extra effort to ensure the item is in tiptop condition. If you later hear the person has sold it on and made a profit that's fine; be glad for them.

Today's thought

MULTI-AGE INTERACTION

Getting to know people from all the generations is interesting, fun and often very touching.

Make an effort to talk to people of all ages. Older people are sometimes scared of youngsters and vice versa, but once you make contact you realize how basically nice other people are, whatever their age.

It's a delight to hear views from a different generation because it gives a fresh perspective and new understanding. It can be really refreshing and very sweet. Enjoy.

Try your hand at being a peace-maker. Soothe away any tensions or disagreements between friends, in the family or in the workplace. Encourage people to resolve differences or find ways to tolerate them. Keep out of others' quarrels and don't take sides. You'll be surprised how often you can gently soothe troubled situations and help people make it up and live happily together again.

Above all, promote a culture where everyone generally gets on well. Remember peace doesn't just happen; it's mostly about intending to live peaceably with each other and doing our best to. A big bonus in making peace is the happiness it brings.

When was the last time you read to someone at bedtime? Children adore being read to and it's good for them, so you feel both appreciated and as though you are doing something worthwhile.

Then there's the joy of the books themselves. Many have fabulous illustrations and stories that are full of deep meaning. Reading to, or being read to, by your partner is also nice and you could consider a children's book again as the good, clear writing is easy to follow even when you're getting sleepy. It's a real pleasure and a happy way to wind down at night.

Live honestly

Live an honest life. Although it can feel good in the moment to steal or cheat, it leaves a pernicious legacy that undermines self-respect and happiness. A clear conscience, on the other hand, is about feeling free and relaxed. To be true to others is to be true to yourself and it enables deep-seated happiness to thrive.

Travel light

Carrying emotional baggage around is exhausting and depressing, so drop it if you can. If you can't, get professional help to go through the various issues so you can loosen hold on them and let them go. Dropping that weight is great. Everyone around you will breathe a sigh of relief, too!

Instant happy

POSTURE
Good posture feels good physically and uplifts your spirits as well as your body.

Adopt the slogan 'glad not glum'. With a toss of your head as you hold it high, shoulders up, spine straight, and decisive, supple movements, you'll instantly grow an inch, feel more confident and have a happier take on the world.

Feeling your solar plexus as your center of gravity will give you great confidence and strength. Walk tall, with a spring in your step, and you'll enjoy whatever you're doing to the full.

When someone's not very nimble-fingered or quick look out for any ways they may appreciate your assistance. Listen for hints carefully, too, as they may not like to ask you directly for help with something. It could be something personal, like giving them a manicure, or technical, such as phoning a utilities company for them and persevering through the endless options! Small things mean such a lot and make you both feel appreciated.

Helping someone with a personal task they can't do for themselves is a Godsend for them and makes you feel good too.

Julie Leggett

327

Showing a readiness to be friendly and neighborly is great for a happy community spirit and lifting people's moods. Is there anyone living nearby who you would like to get to know and who might appreciate your actions? Why not introduce yourself to someone in your neighborhood who you haven't met or hardly know.

You might like to give them your phone number and say, 'Let me know if ever I can be of any help.' Or you could invite them round or ask if you can call on them and arrange a time. If they don't take you up on it, that's OK. It's enough for both you and them to know that you've offered a friendly hand and one day they may have more time to take you up on it.

Don't leave it to the intestacy laws. Make a will and have fun imagining the happiness of all the people you're leaving something to. Enjoy thinking who you'd really like to bequeath something to, or who best deserves it. This could be people who are good to you, relatives and friends, old and maybe new, who you just happen to love, or someone who you know desperately needs a bit of help.

Write plenty of notes to them all, too, to be delivered with your bequests. Tell them you think a lot of them. You'll feel amazingly good; making a will with love in your heart is very, very satisfying.

POTENTIAL ENLIGHTENMENT
Every positive change, however small, has the potential to lead to new enlightenment.

If things aren't being changed the way you think they should, refuse to accept it. Lose the feeling that you have no influence and can't make an impact; you do and you can. Recognize your ability to influence change for the good.

Fight for what's right with all your might. Make 'Lobby, lobby, lobby' your mantra. Like a lever, you can use the tactic of persistence to move mountains of official bodies to make changes few might think possible. Feel powerful. You are.

Planting trees is a wonderful expression of your faith in the future and your love for others and our world (and of course the trees themselves!). They'll take years to mature and may outlive you and that gives a fantastic feeling of continuity and a sense of eternity.

Life goes on and as long as we learn to look after our planet well, hopefully will for billions more years to come. Isn't that a feel-good thought? So plant a tree in your garden or subscribe to a plant-a-tree scheme run by your local park or nature conservation trust. You'll find it really does make you feel happy.

Adopt an 'explorer' attitude in your life. Like an explorer, embrace the challenge of a new idea and enjoy the excitement and fun of finding out how to make it work. It's exciting to explore things. Whether your meanderings are geographical or philosophical, practical or academic, new experiences will keep your mind full of zest.

Say 'Yes' to suggestions often and 'Why not? Let's have a go', even if you're not sure how to do something or how you'll get there. As you make plans the way will become clear. Exploring is profoundly invigorating and often just joyous.

Get up at dawn

Try a new experience: get up at dawn. You'll feel the wonder of the world as it welcomes the light of the day ahead. Each new morning can feel like a miracle all over again.

If you can walk in a garden, park or the countryside, you'll see a magical beauty as the plants and trees are bathed in intensifying light. It's been claimed you can even sometimes see plants' auras (herbs especially) shining around them at this time.

Instant happy

FIRST LIGHT

Getting up at first light gives you a direct line to happiness as you and the world say 'hello' to the new day.

Today's thought

ATONEMENT
Atoning for something
you deeply regret helps
clear the way forward
to happiness.

It feels good to make amends. You know that awful feeling when you've caused damage that can't be undone, no matter how heartfelt your apology?

Atonement is a positive way of making guilt bearable and hopefully, in time, alleviating it. Doing something to help the people concerned or someone or something indirectly affected is a way of bringing a positive out of the mistake or wrong-doing. If you can learn from what happened that feels good, too.

Have a picnic

Eating even the simplest meal outdoors makes it taste like a gourmet's paradise. A picnic is an easy, happy meal, made all the more scrumptious by the fresh air and scenery. Whatever the weather, it's fun, and while it's great to sit on a rug in the sunshine, the more extreme the weather the more welcome the food. Make things easier for yourself by not taking along heavy plates that will need washing up later. It's a holiday, after all!

Take time to pray and meditate; these twin activities are food for the soul. When you are meditating, you are keeping a silent vigil, listening, touching and drawing from a spring of deep peace.

When you are praying, you have conversations with God or, if you prefer, the love that flows through our world. You may find you go from one activity to the other.

Both are like healing oases in our busy, often confusing, lives. Afterward you'll feel better and washed through with happiness.

A long walk, a drive, or a train journey with someone you like can be an unforgettable experience. It offers you both a space in which to talk more deeply, perhaps, or more widely, and certainly for longer than you normally would in one go.

It's also good to share silence as you watch the scenery passing by. Map-reading or navigating roads or stations and ticket systems feels very companionable, too.

Instant happy

GOING SOMEWHERE TOGETHER
Traveling with a friend is a great journey from one place to another in your friendship, too.

Love is happiness, so it's important to appreciate the love you have for others — your friends, family, lover and pets and last but not least God — and theirs for you.

Angela Lloyd-Jones

Loving and being loved is a kind of heaven, but it's so easy not to notice or pay attention to it. Yet love, like any other living thing, needs tender loving care for it to flourish.

Paying attention to your love for others and to theirs for you feels wonderful and with a loving attitude you'll be extra lovable, too. Love is just great, whichever way you look at it. Make your relationships and a loving attitude your top priority. They make happiness thrive.

Be agreeable

day 328

Decide to be agreeable today. However nice you think you are, you'll probably be surprised how many times you have to stop yourself saying, thinking or doing something disagreeable.

It isn't just a case of cutting out snide remarks, selfish thoughts, moans, anger and negative criticism; it's far more about replacing them with kind words, generous thoughts, thanks, peace and praise.

When you remember not to moan and gripe and instead are delightful to yourself and everyone else, your world will automatically sparkle with happiness.

Shake up your happiness

If you tend to forget how good your life is, shake your happiness right up so all the aspects of contentment and joy are there in front of you to be treasured.

Sometimes life, however good, settles into a groove so you don't notice the happiness any more. It's a bit like a down duvet; it needs aerating every now and then. Shaking it up, you'll remember how full of light and joy it is. It keeps you warm and, given the chance, bright and deeply, knowingly, fabulously content.

Happiness does not consist in things, but in the relish we have of them

François duc de la Rochefoucalt

Be a great host

osting is a skill and it's an achievement to be a good host and be able to help others to network. Parties, seminars and any kind of get-together are transformed for you if, instead of waiting anxiously for people to be sociable, you help them.

Get into the habit of introducing people to each other and encouraging them to talk with a conversation-opener to break the ice. You're then free to move on if you wish, joining in established clusters or starting new ones.

Today's thought

WORK ON YOUR CHARISMA

Taking the initiative to put people at their ease feels great and you'll soon have a reputation for being charismatic.

Have a go at engaging fully with life. If you just sit back and let life happen to you, it's all too easy to feel powerless and at the mercy of whatever fate throws at you. But if you actively live the way you want to live now, and think and dream about how you can steer yourself forward the way you want, you'll see how influential you can be.

Set goals, plan and actively take part in making the things and experiences you'd like to happen for real. We're only here once; no time to waste. Enjoy!

When you find a garden you love, just thinking about the happiness you felt there will recall it in a big bear hug of fresh delight. So spend time in your own or your friends' gardens and visit others that are open to the public in your area and beyond, too.

Spending time in a garden will give you a vision and taste of bliss. As well as the sensual delights, it may also be very spiritual. All gardens have a spirit of their own and sometimes, like a beautiful painting, it will resonate with yours, lifting your pleasure to ecstasy.

343

Whenever you need to park the car and can't find a spot, just ask the parking fairy to help you out. She will always find you a space where you want, or pretty close by, except on rare occasions when it wouldn't (for some reason known only to her) be a good idea for you to park there anyway.

As you're approaching the spot, just ask in your mind for a space to be available. Call it crazy if you like, but this tip, goodness knows why, really does work and it gives everyone in the know a great deal of surprised happiness. Just suspend disbelief and try it.

Delegation is an art and the more you practice it, the easier it gets. It shows wisdom and humility to acknowledge that other people can do things as well as you can, sometimes better.

It will please them to be given challenges and responsibilities. And it frees you up to concentrate on the things you really want to do and/or are best at. It's a good leadership skill, and creates a great team dynamic, where you all feel valued and valuable.

Instant happy

TEAMWORK
Share the load and the happiness of working as a team follows.

Whether you tried out several ideas this month or just one, you might like to reflect on what you chose to try and why, and if it worked for you.

1. How many activities did you try this month?

- 1–3 activities ☐
- 4–10 activities ☐
- 11–20 activities ☐
- 21–31 activities ☐

2. How many did you repeat several times in the month?

- 1–3 activities ☐
- 4–10 activities ☐
- 11–20 activities ☐
- 21–31 activities ☐

3. Which activities had a positive effect on your mood this month?

Use the page opposite to make notes about what worked for you and what didn't.

346

Notes, jottings and thoughts

There are plenty of things you are, or could be, really good at. And where there's an ability there's the potential to turn it into a very real talent.

So when you have the wish and potential to do well at something, give it all the energy it needs in order to flourish. Firstly, realize that it's up to you and be positive. Secondly, give it focused, loving attention. Thirdly, devote some energy and effort to learning the skills you need and practicing regularly. This way it's not hard work, it's joyous play.

Reach out

Reach out a friendly hand to someone today. Feeling very emotional, a woman went into a place of worship to gather herself together. The congregation was asked to come and light a candle at the front. Noticing an elderly woman sitting alone she said, 'Would you come up with me?' 'Oh yes' the old lady replied, 'I didn't like to go on my own.' Later they thanked each other, smiling. Neither knew that to each of them the other had seemed like an angel who'd helped lift them out of their blues. You'll feel happy, too, when you become someone's else's angel.

Instant happy

A SMALL GESTURE
Reaching out with a small gesture of friendship can change someone's despair to happiness and hope.

Ponder the meaning of your life and how you can start living in a compatible or complementary way. Think about the work you would like to do or the higher purpose you want to follow.

Just think about what makes you feel right and happy. If it's unrealistic for some unchangeable reason, try thinking sideways. You might, for example, do something else in the same field, or you could make it your special area of study. Either way you'll enjoy the fascination and have the happiness of being involved in something that means a lot to you.

Just for fun, go to a funfair. Yes it's brash and noisy, but hey, it's fun! The loud music, the screams of excitement as people enjoy the rides, the gorgeously gaudy horses on the roundabouts, it all lifts your spirits and makes you laugh. So does eating toffee apples and cotton candy, just like when you were a kid, and trying to snare a prize on one of the competition stalls. Take your courage in your hands, too, and go on one of the fast rides or the big wheel. Brilliant! All the fun of the fair gangs together in an exuberant mixture of excitement and happiness.

day 339   *Break tasks down*

Instant happy

BIT BY BIT
When you move through a job piece by piece, the whole journey feels good.

When you are trying to get something done, it may help to break the project down into easily do-able chunks. Looking at the whole picture can be so daunting that you judder to a halt before you've even begun.

Setting it out in bite-size chunks and tackling them one by one, suddenly makes the process less of a scary task and more of a pleasure. When you complete a section, you'll feel so pleased with yourself you'll eagerly get going with the next one.

When a sunset lights up the sky, revel in it. As the daylight moves westward from your horizon, gaze at the intensifying colors and watch for their peak. You won't know it until it's passed, though, so enjoy every moment, tingling with wonder at the beauty. It's the same in your life. Enjoy the beauty as it comes, arrives and fades, cherishing your happiness.

RIGHTNESS OF PLACE

Love and cherish the rightness of your special place and the feeling of fitting in well with your friends, family and life.

Everyone fits into the world in a unique way. Your personality, characteristics, abilities, work, leisure preferences; each fits individually into the great scheme of things and they dovetail collectively into your special place, too.

Foster the feeling of being truly at home by doing your best, by reaching out to those around you and communicating and connecting with them, by helping out in any way you can. Most of all, be glad you're here and value every day.

Learn from mistakes

Make failures and mistakes a valuable part of your learning curve. We all have them, so don't beat yourself up about yours. They're par for the course. Use them to good advantage as stepping stones back to equilibrium and on to success.

Take rejections in your stride, too. Yes, they hurt. But they also help you flex your muscles and teach you to pace yourself and try again, wiser and stronger. Undaunted, happiness lives again.

Today's thought

SIMPLIFY
Simplify your life so you can enjoy what really matters.

Don't wait until retirement to opt out of the rat race and live the way you want to live. Do it now.

Downshifting and downsizing is all about balancing and uplifting and it's to be applauded. Life isn't about keeping up with the Joneses. What do money and things mean in the great scheme of things? A simpler, less materialistic, life means less worry, more time to yourself, more time with family and friends: more satisfaction.

Try simple and good
day 344

When you're tired or your appetite is jaded, what you need is something that's simple but good. A classic meal, for instance. A boiled free-range egg or two and a slice of wholemeal toast can be a taste of heaven, reminding you how good simple food can be.

Care for yourself
day 345

Look after the whole you with loving, compassionate care. Care for your spirit, too, living in wonder at being part of this world. And nurture all sides of your mind: listen to and value your emotions, develop your brain and embrace your sensuality.

There's something immensely engrossing and feel-good about trying to knock pins down with a swing of your arm and the trajectory of a ball. And when it goes well, homing in just the way you meant, so that, bang, down they go. It just feels so good.

Playing bowls on a green is charmingly gentle and it's good to be out in the open air and daylight. In a different way a game in a bowling alley is satisfying, too. Both kinds have their own special atmosphere and both are great fun.

Go for a swim

Maybe it's time for you to take the plunge. Check out your options at your local swimming pool or a spa, or in the sea, a river or a lake. Swimming is excellent exercise and very comfortable, too, as there are no pressure points on the body.

Swimming also is fun. Just being immersed in the water feels wonderful and swimming gives a great sense of purpose and achievement. Try floating on your back for a while, too. Lying there, with the knowledge that the water will hold you up, feels magical and is really relaxing.

Release creativity

Arrange to have a 'release your creativity day' with a friend or two. You each do whatever appeals to you. For instance, you might like to paint or write, knit, make a soft toy or play with clay; whatever makes you think 'Yes! That's what I'd love to do today!'

Remember, it isn't a competition. It's purely about having fun and inspiration and encouraging each other to follow your own respective enthusiasm, your own special way.

Switch off the auto-pilot and switch on your concentration. You know how easy it is to cruise through the day without really focusing on anything in particular? Make a point today of engaging with what you're doing and what's going on around you.

Your thoughts, reactions and the way you do things are fascinating and so is the body language and behavior of everyone you meet. Take an interest; you'll suddenly feel vibrantly alive and realize you're actively enjoying each moment. You'll have great memories for the end of the day, too.

The key to success is to focus our conscious mind on things we desire not things we fear.

Brian Tracy

When you're revamping a room, follow your heart. Only follow someone else's taste and style if you absolutely adore it. Choose colors and layouts that fit with your conception of your perfect room. Living with someone? That's great. Just take time to find a look that's right for both of you or, if you can't, agree to take turns at being the designer. Surroundings that please you are a steady source of contentment.

Small vexations and imagined or real slights can only take you over if you let them. Prevent them from invading your mind by rationalizing them; tell yourself, for instance, that it isn't important and in the great scheme of things it will all be forgotten sometime soon, or that it's easily dealt with and you don't need to think about it any more right now. To prove you mean it, kick it out now! It feels really good to free up your mind.

Today's thought

GIVE THE BOOT
Give annoying but unimportant grievances the boot. You'll be delighted how much time and happiness you free up.

Protect your time and happiness by refusing to obsess about small things.

Angela Lloyd Jones

NEW HAPPINESS
Welcome new moments
of happiness and the
respite they give you
from sorrow.

Even if you are in the midst of sorrow, keep the thought alive that the return of happiness is possible. It's easy while in despair to scorn the idea that time heals, and certainly grief can last for ever. But usually it lessens at least slightly and if you're prepared to encourage and accept it back into your life, happiness can live side by side with your sorrow. It may not alleviate it, but it will at least interrupt it, giving you moments, or longer periods, of solace. It may enable you, too, to remember the person you've lost and the times you shared with joy.

Adore the magic of Christmas. You may hear people saying that it's lost its appeal? Well it hasn't at all; it's just that they've forgotten the knack of feeling it. If you ever feel disillusioned or disappointed with Christmas, take heart. You can regain all the wonder and fun you enjoyed as a child. Instead of seeing it as a worrying, greedy materialistic splurge, all you have to do is remember the elements of the celebration. Value and enjoy the sharing of happiness, warmth, shelter, food and remember the love of innocence, truth, hope and harmony the season represents. You'll be as rapturous as a child again.

Instant happy

FEEL THE JOY
Christmas is as magical as ever: feel the wonder and the joy.

365

COMING TOGETHER

As you stitch a patchwork quilt, your lives come together in a rich harmony of design and love.

Ever tried patchwork? Why not get together regularly with friends and/or family to make a beautiful quilt? It could be a special commemorative one for a special occasion such as a wedding. It's a splendid project for a group because everyone can choose pieces of fabric they love and enjoy stitching them ready for the quilt and, eventually, into it.

As the work is easy and pleasant, you can all chat. It's interesting to see how your lives develop over the weeks. Your understanding and love for each other will deepen along the way. At the end you'll have a heirloom that's very beautiful, and so precious in the friendship and love it represents, too.

However smart and up to the minute you usually are, keep an old, loose-fitting outfit, or two, to put on for jobs or pastimes where your clothes may get dirty, paint-splattered or otherwise spoilt. Putting them on gets you straight into the right mood and, with no worries about them, you can have a great time getting stuck in. As well as being comfortable, beloved old clothes are comforting: they feel like old friends.

Instant happy

OLD CLOTHES

Save some old clothes for messy jobs or splashing through muddy puddles in the park. They feel great.

THE STRENGTH YOU NEED

You have, or will be given, the strength for whatever you need to accomplish.

If ever your resolve is faltering, just remember how strong you are. You know how plants grow toward the light with an astonishing power? The smallest daisy, for instance, will push through the hardest, stoniest ground to live in the light. Just think of the amazing amount of strength you have.

With the will to follow the path lit up by your guiding star, you'll be just fine. Make your way surely, quietly and happily.

heck out what matters most to you in the current phase of your life. At any particular stage or phase priorities can be different. Romantic relationships, for example, may be all-important at one time of your life and family, studies, work or interests in other periods.

If you need, or want, for a while, to devote a lot of energy to one aspect of your life, go with the flow of it. Recognizing where your priorities lie and what your needs are now, you can juggle the various aspects of your life realistically and comfortably, enjoying them all.

Today's thought

REPLENISH
Adjust your life according to your current needs and priorities to replenish happiness constantly.

369

day 358 — *You are significant*

Instant happy

JUST SING
Sing with happiness at the privilege of being alive and able to make a difference.

Every thought, word, hope, from the smallest thing you do to the biggest achievements, has an effect on the world that may be far greater than you realize. Isn't that amazing? Doesn't it make you aware of how vital it is to do your best, live as well as you can, and, above all, be a transmitter of love, goodwill and happiness?

So, yes, you are significant. Whatever happens to the human race over the next billion years, your presence now can make a difference somehow, somewhere in this dimension and perhaps others.

Everything we do has a ripple effect that goes right around the world and, who knows, probably beyond it in other dimensions.

John Avenel Rench

Use the supports available as you come through sorrow or depression. There is much wisdom and comfort to be found in books and in talking with a counselor or trusted friend. Prayer and meditation are very healing. Pets are terrific sources of love, support and joy. Nature can be soothing, too. Exercise and good food boost feel-good serotonin. Loving sex or simply affectionate touch release endorphins, another natural chemical that gives a warm, lasting glow. So take courage; there is much help available to you. Sense the love and healing power flowing around and through you and feel how good that is.

Be a provider

Be a hunter-gatherer or homemaker. Following in our ancient ancestors' traditions and bearing their gene imprint too, we are geared up to provide for ourselves.

So skip the thought that continuous idleness or holidays would be brilliant; it wouldn't at all. You'd only have the nagging, unsettling feeling that something was missing. Be glad to follow your purpose in life, be it work, parenting, homemaking, caring for others or keeping busy with your interests. Enjoy the enriching sense of continuity and belonging it gives you.

Nice as it is to conform most of the time, it's great to surprise yourself and others now and then. You could, for example, wear something outrageous, or go against your usual type and be really introvert or extrovert instead.

Changing your own and other people's perception of you, even in a short, one-off way, gives your spirits a big charge of happiness. Being crazily different is fun!

> *Surprise yourself and others and free your inner sense of fun.*
>
> Peter Gregory

373

Do something extra-loving today; something you normally wouldn't do. You could, for instance, as well as doing your household chores, surprise your partner by doing one or two of theirs as well. You could be especially affectionate or say something that will make them feel terrific. Or you could do a kindness for a neighbor, co-worker, stranger or friend totally out of the blue. Remember it's in addition to what you'd normally do anyway, so push the boundaries, go the extra distance and just love how good it feels.

Start a book or music club in your neighborhood. It's fun to get together with a few friends, old or new, on a regular basis. If you love reading, a book club is a great incentive to read more widely than you usually would and it's great to compare thoughts and reactions.

A music club is total bliss as you simply sit back and listen to the selections and it's great to hear music that's new to you as well as old favorites you're already familiar with. It feels good to take turns at choosing and talking and to enjoy the happy atmosphere of sharing an interest.

day 364 — *Look at the view*

Today's thought

THE VIEW
Stopping to take in the view is part of the joy of any climb.

Whenever you're climbing, pause frequently to admire the view. Whether you are actually walking up a hill or climbing a career ladder, learning a new skill or progressing a project, it feels good to put your energy enthusiastically into the effort. But taking frequent breaks will re-energize you. And if you turn around and take in the scenery, both distant views and your immediate surroundings, you'll appreciate the beauty of it all and see how far you've come, too. It's so important to look back at what you've achieved; it makes every journey happier.

376

Make peace

Make your peace with the past year and welcome the new one ahead. Choose to make it rich with love and interest. Remember you have tremendous ability to learn from, and adapt to, changes and new experiences and to develop your mind. Scientists have found that we humans use only a fraction of the brain's capacity, so just think how satisfying it will be to use even a little bit more of your own. Life is full of scope and promise.

Instant happy

ENJOY
Enjoy the beauty, the wonder, the love. the potential. Go for it!

Whether you tried out several ideas this month or just one, you might like to reflect on what you chose to try and why, and if it worked for you.

1. How many activities did you try this month?

- 1–3 activities
- 4–10 activities
- 11–20 activities
- 21–31 activities

2. How many did you repeat several times in the month?

- 1–3 activities
- 4–10 activities
- 11–20 activities
- 21–31 activities

3. Which activities had a positive effect on your mood this month?

Use the page opposite to make notes about what worked for you and what didn't.

Notes, jottings and thoughts

Conclusion

Happiness – is it about attitude, luck or science? Whether you read this book straight through or dip in, the suggested ways to happiness show it's very much a mixture of all three.

Life! For all of us, is a varied journey. Sometimes it's sunny and bright, sometimes dark and cheerless. Mostly it chugs along in the middle. But always you have the innate ability to choose your attitude. Think positive and you'll home in on any silver lining. At the same time, you'll release feel-good chemicals in your brain and body, helping you to be calmer, stronger and ultimately happier. Often, you'll invite good fortune into your life. As you practice the positive-thinking habit, you'll increasingly often feel happy. Take time to notice good feelings and consciously enjoy them. By welcoming them, you'll encourage them to stay longer and visit you more often.

It's all too easy to forget to be positive, so keep this book handy to dip into for ways to get back on the happiness path. Remember Julian of Norwich's words 'All shall be well and all manner of things shall be well.'

Notes, jottings and thoughts

Notes, jottings and thoughts